HOW TO
ASK
FOR
MONEY

To Dr. Lyon,

HOW TO
ASK
FOR
MONEY

THE MOST IMPORTANT RULES AND FORMULAS
OF AN AWARD WINNING FUNDRAISER

ALANA STOTT, MBE

ARCHWAY
PUBLISHING

Archway Publishing books may be ordered
through booksellers or by contacting:

Archway Publishing
1663 Liberty Drive
Bloomington, IN 47403
www.archwaypublishing.com
844-669-3957

ISBN: 978-1-6657-3660-2 (sc)
ISBN: 978-1-6657-3659-6 (hc)
ISBN: 978-1-6657-3661-9 (e)

Library of Congress Control Number: 2023900543

Print information available on the last page.

Archway Publishing rev. date: 3/16/2023

PART 4: EXTRAS

INTRODUCTION
WHAT IS MOTIVATING YOU?

As far back as I can remember, I've been motivated by two things:

HELPING PEOPLE AND MAKING MONEY.

Now, what is your first thought when I say I'm motivated by money? Is your mind suddenly flooded with the lyrics of **Kanye West's song "Gold Digger"**? Do you think of Michael Douglas on the set of *Wall Street*? Or maybe you imagine **Scrooge McDuck** blowing gold coins straight out of his beak!

I imagine whatever you're envisioning is less Mother Teresa and more Donald Trump. Perhaps you think it makes me ruthless or possibly cold—more than likely not very welcoming. So before you form the wrong impression, let me explain further. My life is about **fulfilling my**

purpose, which is helping others and motivating people to be the best they can be.

$ $ $

I learned two lessons very early on in life.

THE FIRST WAS THAT THERE ARE A LOT OF PEOPLE OUT THERE WHO NEED HELP.

THE SECOND WAS THAT I HAD THE ABILITY TO HELP PEOPLE.

I've always had a head for numbers, and from a young age I've been driven by targets and goals. I love taking on new challenges—

THE TOUGHER THE BETTER.

My dad used to tell me I wasn't made for the mundane. I thrived in high-pressure environments, but helping people was what really gave me a buzz. I soon realized that money was a big contributing—if not the main—factor in helping others. In order to help people, one needs resources, and those usually come at a cost. Making money became a big part of my life for that reason.

Making money was one thing, but what about asking for it? I knew that if I could perfect the asking, I'd be able to take my desire to help others to new heights. I could already help many people with what I earned myself, but asking others to contribute to causes would definitely increase my ability to reach new levels. There really wouldn't be any limits to what I could achieve. The better I became at asking others to contribute, the more and more people I could help.

$ $ $

I BEGAN WORKING AT THE TENDER AGE OF ELEVEN.

My mom was a single parent, and she herself worked three jobs. There was no spare income, so if we wanted anything, we had to work for it.

My first job was working in a railway café. They told me I was too young to be on the payroll, but they gave me food to take home. The food was good—better than what we could afford, so I did the work. I may have been getting paid with food, but I was able to use the experience to learn everything I could about working.

By the time I turned twelve, I was being paid with money. I began by earning £1.50 ($1.80) per hour, but I worked hard and soon pushed that up to £2.00 ($2.40) per hour.

By the age of thirteen I was working two jobs: one in a fast-food place and the other in tele-marketing. Telemarketing was a high-pressure sales environment, and it was there I learned about the fine art of selling. This business was all about targets, goals, and achievements.

I was paid £2 per hour plus commission on my sales, and I learned quickly how money was made. The more I sold, the more I earned. After I lost my mother at fifteen, I was more driven than ever to earn. I not only had to look after myself; I also had a young brother to care for, bills to pay, and food to put on the table.

I was offered a job as a traveling salesperson when I was eighteen. The pay was fully com-mission, but the earnings were unlimited—that was the upside. But that also meant that if I didn't sell, I didn't earn anything at all.

IN MY LIFE, THE BUCK HAS ALWAYS STOPPED WITH ME.

I haven't had backups or people to support me. If I didn't hustle, if I didn't sell, I didn't eat—it was that simple. If you've ever been in the position where you had to choose between buying food or paying the electricity bill, you know the only thing you want to take from that situation is the knowledge that you never want to be in it again.

People's basic human needs are often met by others when they are children. Most are nourished and kept healthy, warm, clothed, and sheltered by their parents. As people grow, they learn how to take care of these needs themselves, but they have the knowledge that someone's there to back them up if they struggle.

Too many children, however, don't ever have those needs met by someone else, even at young ages. They have to learn quickly how to keep warm and find food and shelter for themselves. They know they don't have anyone to turn to, and they understand **the fear**—the fear that if they can't get food, they won't eat. If they can't find warmth, they'll stay cold. If they can't find shelter, they won't be safe.

THEY KNOW ALL TOO WELL THAT THE BUCK STOPS FIRMLY WITH THEM.

These kids don't have safety nets, but what they do have—what they have built over the years—is an abundance of steely resilience. Money can become their motivator, as it ensures their basic needs are met. For people like me, they also want to help others who haven't been able to have those needs met and have no one to turn to.

Money however, is not always a person's prime motivator, and it's important to establish what motivates other people in their lives.

WHAT ARE THEIR DRIVING FORCES?

WHAT ARE THEIR REASONS FOR GETTING OUT OF BED EVERY DAY?

You may think this is just a requirement in business or of the management team, but I'm here to tell you: if you can establish this in all situations with all the people in your life, getting what you want will suddenly become a whole lot easier. This is true in business, in relationships, and in friendships. Basically, if you know what motivates any person you're interacting with, you immediately have the upper hand in any given situation.

$ $ $

At nineteen I was offered a great job in finance that allowed me to stop having to knock on doors for a living. It too was commission-based, but it came with a much higher salary. I immediately jumped at the chance to work with this company, and within six months I'd been promoted to supervisor and then manager not long after that.

My first mistake was thinking everyone was like me. I thought everyone's drives were the same—that we all had the same desires. (That's how you know what your true motivators are: you struggle to understand that everyone else isn't motivated by them.) My belief that everyone was motivated by money was my first and biggest mistake.

THIS BELIEF SERVED AS A BLOCKAGE IN MY MINDSET.

For example, when I needed to motivate the young single guys on my sales team to work harder, I could flash the prospect of earning extra cash at them, and they'd almost always jump at it. But then I had an employee I'll call Margaret, a forty-eight-year-old mother of three whose first grandchild had just arrived.

She was planning her annual family holiday to Spain while thinking of what food she had to put in the oven that evening—those were her priorities—and my job became a lot harder. The promise of riches did nothing to entice this lady to work late into the night.

Margaret worked to pay the bills, and once she'd done that, all she wanted to do was spend time with her family. She paid her bills precisely on time every month and worked from the exact hours of nine to five, Monday through Friday. She did her job well, but work did not cross her mind once in the evenings, on the weekends, or during her four weeks of holiday each year.

If I wanted to pry extra work, or even optimum performance, from Margaret, **the color of money would never work**; in fact, trying to lure her with money could cause her to feel contempt. From her perspective, she couldn't understand why anyone would have a prime driving force that didn't include spending time with loved ones. Her motivator was so strong in her mind that all other motivators confused her as much as people not being motivated by money con-fused me.

One evening I was settling myself into the office for another round of excessive overtime. I'd received nothing but dirty looks from Margaret for the past year or so whenever I'd told her that her dreams should be bigger. That if she worked harder, she could swap her annual family trip to Spain for a trip to the Maldives. That she could have it all if she just tried harder. I watched that evening as Margaret began her end-of-day routine.

At five o'clock on the dot, her coat was on, her desk—always immaculate—had been tidied, her computer was shut down, and she was out the door, same as always. On this evening she seemed particularly keen saying goodbye to any potential bonus that would have come with extra hours worked. As she hurried away, I shook my head and **rolled my eyes** at her lack of discipline and motivation.

I got up to switch on the lights (winter evenings in Scotland are dark and dreary). I popped on the coffee pot for my evening pick-me-up, and as I waited for it to warm up, I looked outside at the winter's evening. The snow had begun to fall, and the streetlights were sparkling on the ground. Everyone out there was in warm coats, leaving their offices and heading out to start Christmas shopping or to meet friends for drinks.

RIGHT AT THAT MOMENT, I LEARNED A LESSON THAT FOREVER CHANGED MY LIFE.

As I looked out, all alone from my first-floor window, the smell of my freshly brewed coffee stimulating the office air, I saw Margaret practically sprinting across the road, arms fully extended, looking like she was ready to take on Usain Bolt in the hundred-meter final.

Her excitement was evident in the wide smile that stretched across her face. She was beaming so incredibly, and it was definitely a new look to me. This enthusiastic woman didn't look anything like the slouching, half-bored, clock-watching one I was used to seeing in the office. No, this was more like Jeff Bezos when he first heard mandatory lockdowns were being extended worldwide—she was *genuinely* ecstatic. My eyes moved from my newly gleaming coworker to the target of her enthusiasm, and everything suddenly became abundantly clear to me.

There, waiting patiently outside in the snow, was Margaret's daughter and brand-new grandchild. She scooped that baby up in her arms and pulled her daughter close to kiss her on the forehead. She snuggled the baby close to her chest in a way that suggested she had been waiting an eternity for that moment. She placed the baby gently back into her stroller, tucked her up nice and warm, then wrapped her arm snugly through her daughter's. They walked off into the falling snow arm-in-arm, pushing the stroller together.

In that instant I understood she would not think about work again until she sat back at her desk on Monday morning. *This* was her motivation. *This* is why she got up in the morning and fought her way through her work—to get to that five o'clock moment. This is her driving force. **I realized then and there I could never motivate her with my drives;** however, by understanding what drove her I could approach her in a way that would make sense to her. My entire work-place narrative and how I motivated Margaret changed from that day forth.

Following this revelation and onto when I became a bank manager, one of the first things I worked on was establishing what the primary driving force of each and every member of my workforce was. I needed to know what motivated them to get out of bed every day, and I used those drivers to get them to be their most productive selves.

If I had tried to inspire them using my motivators or tried to change their drive, it would never have resonated with them. I had to use their passions that already burned brightly within them.

SO WHAT ARE THE PRIME MOTIVATORS WITHIN PEOPLE?

In my experience there are **eight key motivators.** Of course these can be subcategorized, and there are always the obscure and unusual ones; however, for now I will stick with the main ones.

$ **Power**

$ **Self-growth**

$ **Recognition and approval**

$ **Winning**

$ **Helping other people**

$ **Money**

$ **Passion**

$ **Time with loved ones**

DO YOU KNOW WHAT MOTIVATES YOU?

WHAT ARE THE PRIME MOTIVATORS OF THE PEOPLE AROUND YOU?

If you're unsure, you can work this out for yourself very simply by numbering each of the eight motivators according to their order of importance to you.

Take each motivator and compare it to the next. It is important you be 100 percent honest with yourself in each answer and that you answer with no self-judgment. Answer from your heart and gut, and don't second-guess yourself.

ASK YOURSELF WHETHER POWER IS MORE IMPORTANT TO YOU THAN SELF-GROWTH.

If it is, put that at number one for now. If it isn't, it goes to number two, and self-growth is number one.

Next look at recognition and approval. Is that more important to you than your number two? If so, move it to number two, and move your two to three. If it has become your number two, then do the same exercise with your number one. If recognition is more important than your number one, then move it to number one, and your number one will now sit in the two spot.

Do this with every motivator. Don't rush. Spend time on each one, understanding what each means and looks like. Feel what it would feel like to have each one, and focus on the importance. By the end of the exercise, you will have a list of your own motivators. Your top two will be the driving forces for much of what you do and will determine how you make your decisions.

ONCE YOU KNOW WHAT MOTIVATES YOU, YOU CAN MOVE ON TO THE PEOPLE AROUND YOU.

If you are unsure, spend time with them. Play board games and chat to them about their goals and dreams. Really listen and absorb what they say. Once you master this, you will very quickly be able to work it out for any new people that come into your life.

You can apply this method when you are in a position of asking people for money. Working out what is motivating them will help you develop your pitch to ask them for a donation or to invest in your idea or support your cause or journey. You want to know what motivates them and also what the motivations and goals of any of their companies are.

There are many reasons people give money to others. They believe in the cause, or it might help their business. It could make them feel or look good or help them curry favor with others. The list is long and extensive, but the number one reason people give money to other people is ...

BECAUSE THEY WERE ASKED!

It's as simple as that. If you want the investment in your idea, the donation to your cause, or even the overpriced designer handbag, I promise you will be at least one step closer to getting it by simply asking. How big that step is and how close you are to receiving it will depend on many factors.

I'm not talking about whether the benefactor is having a good day or not. The factors involved will be the work *you* have put in prior to the ask. It is this pre-work that will determine the outcome of the ask every single time.

THIS IS THE VERY REASON ASKING FOR MONEY IS ONE OF THE MOST FEARED, UNCOMFORTABLE, AND ACTIVELY AVOIDED TASKS ON ANYONE'S TO-DO LIST.

Fear of rejection, awkward unknowns, and a complete lack of preparation are factors that drive most people to sweaty palms, heart palpitations, and running for the nearest exit. But there is no getting away from the fact that, for most businesses and certainly nonprofits, financing, investment, and donations are the most essential aspects of their operations and are what will determine the successes of their campaigns. These fears and unknowns are what drive many companies to enlist the help of expert fundraising and investment firms.

Why do people find it so difficult to ask for money?

FEAR AND THE UNKNOWN

Why do companies choose to hire specialized consultants to do this job?

They see the consultants' confidence and believe in their knowledge. Projecting confidence and having knowledge is great, but how does it benefit your company's future if all this wisdom stays with the consultants? It would be best for you if they instead taught others the methods.

Of course, this is the business of fundraising consultants. They don't want to give away trade secrets. The magician doesn't break the rules of the magic circle. The issue lies in hiring a consultant who is not fully up to the job. Before long, questions arise.

When hiring a funding consultant for businesses or nonprofits, some of the most frequent complaints are:

$ Why isn't the money coming in?

$ Why isn't the money coming in faster?

$ Why isn't the committee doing their job?

$ Why aren't the introducers bringing in business?

$ Why are we losing donors?

$ Why are the donors saying no?

$ Should we go on hold until the economy gets better?

$ Should we lower our goals?

$ What are we paying you for anyway?

The answer to all these issues can be found before the process has even begun. In fact, about **90 percent of the work required to produce a successful pitch or ask for money happens well before you even step foot near that boardroom or meeting place.**

Therefore, hiring a consultant at the eleventh hour or for specific pitches may be successful a small portion of the time, but for ultimate sustained success, the fundraising consultant would have to either become an integral part of your structure or teach you everything they know.

OVER THE COURSE OF THIS BOOK, I AM GOING TO DO JUST THAT.

I am breaking every rule of the magic circle and sharing with you all I've learned in my twenty-plus years of asking for money. I will guide you through the process of what should happen during this 90 percent window and teach you my uniquely formulated, tried-and-tested method to put into practice my key steps to success. I will take you seamlessly through all aspects of your fundraising process and help you become comfortable asking for money.

$ $ $

My proven system has helped businesses and non-profits raise millions of dollars. My aim is that upon finishing this book, you'll have all the resources and knowledge you need to approach your donors with confidence and deliver successful pitches.

Asking for money is a skill I believe we all need, and if you're reading this —congratulations! You have taken your first step and completed your first lesson in becoming a master at fundraising. Now it's time to learn the recipes and secrets to success.

Are you ready?

LET'S GO!

HOW TO
ASK
FOR
MONEY

PART ONE

DOUBTS AND FEARS

CHAPTER ONE

HOW NOT TO ASK FOR MONEY

When learning how to ask for money, one of the first lessons you must understand is

HOW NOT TO DO IT.

Believe me when I say there are many methods that will have even the kindest donors running for the hills, their cash still firmly in-hand. Even with the best intentions, a fundraiser can make a number of common mistakes when approaching a donor or investor. It's important we address these before learning how to actually ask for money.

Let's look at what has led you to this moment in which you're asking someone for money. You have taken the time to come up with your idea. You've possibly spent years being passionate about a cause, or told all your mates you're going to do something amazing and raise loads of money doing it. You've spent sleepless nights thinking about it, reading books, studying, dreaming, and googling, and now you are ready to start.

When growing an established business, starting a new endeavor, or working for a good cause, the first fundamental necessity is access to capital and funding. This stage of the process makes you feel like you're really making things happen, so you immediately begin the process of finding donors.

You start with cold calls, friends of friends, pins in a map, posts on social media, and often attempting to get celebrity or press interest. You walk into rooms, post long heartfelt messages, send out newsletters, and knock on doors, ready to start watching the money roll in. You're excited to share all about why you're pursuing this path, what you are going to do, and how hard you have worked to get there.

You have seen so many of these campaigns online get funded, so with a cause as good as yours this should be easy, right?

Have you ever experienced a job interview in which you were asked a question along the lines of,

"SO WHAT DO YOU KNOW ABOUT OUR ORGANIZATION?"

They're not asking this question to be sure you know the current stock price or the staff retention ratio for the last three years. They ask this question because they want to know how much time you have taken to prepare, how much research you have put in, and how much you want *this* job. They do not care that you have been out of work for the past three months, have applied for two hundred jobs, and right now will work for *anyone* doing *anything* to pay the bills. They want to know this exact job is the job you want. This is the company you want to work for, and you are willing to put the homework in to make it happen.

It's no different when you are mixing in the world of investment and raising capital. No investor wants to receive a mass email starting with, **Dear Sir**—particularly when said investor is not, in fact, a sir. Each individual wants to know he or she is special and has been chosen by you to invest in this opportunity.

Later on, we will go deeper into this topic to ensure you're fully prepared for the investment version of, "What do you know about our organization?"

Another huge pet peeve for investors and do-nors is when an ask is obviously for personal gain. You may be thinking, *What? If you're asking for money, surely it's always for gain!* That is true to an extent, but the investors don't want to know what you will personally gain. They want to see what gain there will be for their industry, what commercial growth there will be for them, and what success they will see within their own portfolio.

The donor wants to see a gain for the cause, for their corporate social responsibility (CSR), or for any of the other reasons they may consider your proposal. But the one thing I can categorically guarantee is that if an investor or donor believes you are doing this only for your own personal financial gain, even if that is not the case, you will most likely fill them with doubt and lose their investment.

This may sound confusing, so let me give an example. I was once approached to help with a charity exhibition. One of my first asks was to review the fundraiser's budget plan, in which I discovered they had almost $250k in expenses. A quick google of their planned exhibition revealed the average cost of such an event was around $75k, so I asked what the remaining $175k was for. Their reply was a vague reference to "costs and stuff."

OK?

Alarm bells rang immediately, so I delved further. I needed to know what this "stuff" was. I think they thought they would ask me for help raising the money, give me the figures, and I would go and get it. Unfortunately for them, this is a business, my business, and I treat it as such, as will donors and investors. They have earned this money you are asking for, and they want to know exactly where it's going. I continued to go deeper with them, and they eventually divulged it was for flights, hotels, food, and so forth.

This was meant to be a five-day event for three people. So again, I pressed that $175k for flights and food just did not make sense. After a few more probing questions from me and several sweaty palms for them, they told me it was to cover their own out-of-pocket expenses. They figured that since they were taking time off work to raise money for charity, it would be OK for them to get paid for it.

There it was—the truth. But by this point they had lost one of the key elements I require to work with someone:

INTEGRITY.

Were they wrong to want compensation for what they were doing? Absolutely not. Their failing came when they tried to hide their own gains within other costs. They weren't being honest, and they had compromised trust in the partnership.

The correct way to move forward would be to add the real numbers into their budget plan if they felt the costs were necessary. Then potential donors have the opportunity to discuss the price and decide whether to pay it or not. They may very well decide the proposal is fair, or they may decide the ask is too much and want to negotiate. Either way, you still have their trust because you told them the full truth.

But when you lose trust and the donor thinks you lack integrity, your deal will more than likely be all over.

$ $ $

Another huge mistake can come in the form of a

LOSS OF DIGNITY.

Sometimes you have put in all the hard work. You've done your research, and you gave the performance of a lifetime in your pitch. All your figures are nailed, and you've displayed your absolute all. You are so sure the investor will say yes that you're already planning champagne celebrations in your head.

But unfortunately, after listening to everything you have said, the investor you just pitched decides your idea isn't right for him at this time. Your emotions are already at a boiling point, and your excitement has now turned to anger and disappointment. You want to yell, scream, and name call. However, this is the exact point where you must say,

"THANK YOU VERY MUCH FOR YOUR TIME AND CONSIDERATION. IF YOU RECONSIDER, I'D LOVE TO HEAR FROM YOU, BUT FOR NOW I'M INCREDIBLY GRATEFUL YOU TOOK THE TIME TO ALLOW ME TO HIGHLIGHT THIS OPPORTUNITY."

You could even ask for feedback that might help you in the future. But what you absolutely *do not* do is start a debate or argument. You don't demand to know why or ask for full reasoning or an explanation. Stamping your feet and overreacting emotionally will only serve to make this potential investor never allow you through the door again.

Any number of reasons could have impacted his decision to reject your pitch—one of those being timing. If you throw your toys out of the pram and cause a fuss, that moment of bad timing will easily cause permanent damage.

$ $ $

The next mistake is one of the most common. It's taking advantage of people because you believe

THEY'RE RICH, SO WHY NOT.

I have a business acquaintance and friend who is a very prominent and successful businessman in the oil and gas industry. He was self-made and worked incredibly hard. He was also a very generous man. He was known about town as the man who always settled the bill. He was always paying for events, supporting his friends' business ventures, and generally looking after those he loved. Then in 2016 the oil and gas crisis hit in the North Sea, and his income took a huge hit.

It wasn't long before he wasn't able to settle the bills anymore, and he had to start saying no to people. He told me this was when he really saw people's true colors and learned who his real friends were. When he was no longer their cash machine, they were not only no longer his friends, they were also bad-mouthing him to everyone who would listen.

They had become so used to him saying yes that when he did have to say no to them, he became tantamount to the devil. Needless to say, it was a steep learning curve for him. But, as the self-made man he was, it wasn't long until he was back on his feet. And as sure as the sun will rise every day, the swarm of so-called friends returned to give it another try. However, his memory had not faded. He remembered who had walked through the cloudy times with him and who had run for the hills.

When it comes to a person's hard-earned money, it is completely their decision as to whether or not they agree to the funding, just as it is completely your decision as how you react to their choice. You can burn bridges and cut every tie, or you can thank them for the opportunity, take away any lessons from the pitch, and retain a chance for a future pitch. Respect is key. No one owes you anything, and remembering that will get you very far.

Finally, without any shadow of a doubt, the worst thing you can do to an investor when you are asking for their money is to continually point out anything from the following list in your pitch.

1. How much money the donor has.
2. How easily the donor can afford it.
3. How the ask is nothing to them.
4. How it's the right thing to do.

These statements are all not only rude, but they also show a complete lack of respect for the donor. How much money they have, if they can afford it, how little the ask is to them, or what is right for them, is **100 percent** their business and zero percent yours. The attitude that someone can afford it; therefore, they should give it to you is an incredibly entitled attitude and a big turn-off to investors.

This shows a bad attitude and laziness on your part, but it also gives the donor deep insight into how you will handle business going forward. Whether this is for a business or non-profit, it isn't an attitude that bodes well for you or your future fundraising.

I have had firsthand experience with this example of **how not to ask for money**. My mother had the kindest heart and would do anything for anyone. Even as a single mother working three jobs, she always had time to help other people. She died when I was fifteen, and it wasn't until much later in life that I realized how much of an influence she had been on me. I had relatives who did not inherit her kind heart and often displayed an **entitled attitude**.

I visited my cousin in the hospital following the birth of her first child. We weren't a close family, but this was a new baby. I picked up a beautiful baby-boy hamper and came up to the hospital to see the gorgeous new arrival.

One of my relatives was there, and as I placed the hamper down and went to hug the new mama, my dear sweet old aunt who was sitting there commented on how beautiful the gift was.

My other relative snipped back, **"Whatever, she can afford it."**

I turned around in disbelief and felt immediately deflated. She saw someone she perceived to be flaunting money and trying to make them feel bad. It was as though she felt it was my duty to do this since her entitled mind believed I could afford to.

What never crosses these entitled minds are the hours, days, months, and years of hard work, sacrifice, hustle, and grind that came before this moment. The sleepless nights, the failures, the loneliness, and the moments of complete exhaustion. Watching others having fun while you keep building your little empire, sacrificing carefree times, and watching others take home secure paychecks every week while you're out there risking it all. No, all they see is the final result.

Much like how I felt that day in the hospital, investors feel deflated when they hear words like "*you can afford it*" in a pitch, and their years of hard work feel completely unappreciated. This is not a good way to make anyone feel, but they have something you want! When they hold the power and you make them feel like that, you may as well leave, and then take a long, hard look at yourself.

SUMMARY

$ Don't walk into a room without knowing your audience.

$ Don't make things up, pretend you know, or fudge figures.

$ Do accept no for an answer.

$ Don't disrespect your potential investors and donors.

CHAPTER TWO

HOW NOT TO RECEIVE MONEY

I want you to think about Christmas. It's a special time—one of joy, merriment, carol-singing, and gift-giving. Your mom is having the whole family around, so you pack up the car with gifts and start the journey to see the oldies. The car is filled with excitement and treats wrapped in Christmas paper, decorated in silver bows and tinsel.

My most-treasured part of Christmas is now approaching: handing out the treats and watching people's faces as they open the gifts I carefully selected for them. It fills me with absolute joy and happiness to give gifts and watch as they make others smile.

During the car ride, I also practice my grateful face. This is mainly for the tiny members of the family who have handmade some crafty little number, or the over-nineties who have carefully giftwrapped those gray socks with oh-so-much love. They are feeling every bit of excitement that I am feeling about watching loved ones open their gifts.

So what happens when someone hasn't practiced their "Wow, what an amazing gift" face? What if dear old Granny hands over the gift-wrapped socks to the stroppy fifteen-year-old, who looks at them with total contempt and throws them to the ground, exclaiming how lame this all is? All the joy, anticipation, and excitement disappears from Granny's eyes. She tries to mask her hurt, as all her effort in giving this gift has gone completely unappreciated.

It crushes her, but chances are sweet old Granny will not give up. Next year she will wrap that gift again with just as much love and care, with the hope this year it will be loved.

YOUR LOVELY GRANNY MAY BE THIS SWEET AND FORGIVING, BUT THAT'S NOT LIKELY TO BE TRUE FOR DONORS.

When a donor doesn't feel loved or appreciated chances are their first donation will be their last. When we take money without giving thanks, without showing real gratitude and appreciation, what we are saying to the donor is,

"YOU HAVE SERVED YOUR PURPOSE. I GOT WHAT I WANT, AND NOW I DON'T NEED YOU".

I once planned a fundraisier that was an inaugural event for a very high-profile nonprofit at a prestigious venue in Scotland. This was a charity I was an ambassador for, so I was not charging for my services. I spent nine months planning the event, organizing everything from start to finish. I organized all the sponsors, donors, auction prizes, entertainment, and guests. I was also almost eight months pregnant the day of the event.

The day started at six in the morning. I had to prepare the hotel for the arrival of the guests, some arriving by air, all who were being collected by a fleet of Bentleys I had secured on loan for the day.

We had some amazing guests, some very generous donors, and by the end of the day, an incredible event. The event was very successful, for the most part down to our wonderful main sponsor who footed the bill for most of the costs. These types of sponsors are like gold and should be cherished.

A full sponsor enables an event to start off in the green immediately, which always makes hitting fundraising targets a lot easier. (I delve into this more in chapter 15.) The night ended around 2 a.m., and my feet had completely swollen after being on them all night. I was so exhausted when I got to the hotel room, I planted my large pregnant body onto the bed and fell asleep, evening dress still on!

The next morning I awoke, my feet so swollen I could barely stand up. My husband had to help me to the bathroom, and all attempts at getting dressed were futile. My mind and body were completely exhausted, and no matter how much I tried, I wasn't able to go down to the lobby to wave goodbye to the overnight guests. However, I knew the group from the non-profit were there, so I had faith they would say all the goodbyes and thank-yous to the sponsors and donors as they departed.

After I returned home, I began sorting through the post-event admin—an incredibly important aspect of event planning, if not the most important part. I issued the charity with all the prizewinners and supplied them with the completed lists. It was then in their hands to send out the event information, including the totals raised and thank-you notes. My job was done, and I could relax. A short while after this I had my baby, and it wasn't long until the charity's big London event was due to take place.

One afternoon I received a call from my main sponsor from the inaugural event. He was not happy. He had just received an email from the charity asking him what auction prizes he wished to offer for the main event and if he would consider being a sponsor. This sponsor was incredibly generous—well-known for his generosity. The prizes he donated to charities often fetched in the tens if not hundreds of thousands of dollars. But on this call, he was beyond furious.

He told me that following the Scotland event he had not heard anything from the charity. No one had been there when he departed the hotel, and he had heard nothing from them until this letter, begging him for more generosity.

Despite him covering the costs of the Scottish event and donating major prizes, they had not taken the time to send him a simple letter of gratitude. He had heard of other donors, more local to the charity headquarters, being invited to garden parties and dinners, yet he had not even been given the courtesy of a thank-you card. Now they were getting in touch with another ask. Needless to say, he was no longer interested in supporting the charity.

This is an exact example of **how not to receive money.** If you are not prepared to show gratitude and appreciation to your donor, then you should expect they will not return, and rightly so. Who wants to feel unappreciated and used for what people can get from them? The old saying, "Fool me once, shame on you; fool me twice, shame on me," applies to this situation. The charity lost this donor, when they could have kept him for the price of a thank-you card.

$ $ $

It should go without saying that no business or non-profit should accept investments or donations that they know or suspect has come from an illegal source. This type of transaction amounts to money laundering or is being donated immorally.

But what about when the transaction is not quite hitting the bar of the definition of illegal? What if it just *feels* wrong? I am a firm believer in listening to your gut. Mine has never failed to give me the answers. Even when I have chosen to ignore it, it's always proven to be right.

In 2018 museums were heavily criticized for accepting donations from the Sackler family. The family, who own Purdue Pharma, had faced lawsuits and criticism over alleged over-prescribing of pharmaceuticals such as Oxycontin, an addictive prescription drug responsible for a large number of overdose deaths in the United States. Campaigners believed the museums were allowing themselves to become a moral cover to sweeten the negative chatter about the family.

In this day and age of social media, guilt by association is a big worry for corporations and nonprofits alike. It's important any decisions made by donors and beneficiaries align exactly with what the company believes in and stands for.

A human-trafficking organization spoke with me about bringing on a new ambassador, who was sponsored by a large sportswear company that was infamous for their poor practices in combatting forced labor and sweatshops. While the individual was passionate about joining the fight, my advice was the association with this ambassador would do more damage than good. For a charity to retain trust and integrity with its supporters, it is so important that everything they align themselves with meet their values. Selling out for the payday will ultimately do damage to the brand or cause and often cause damage that is irreparable.

Another big no-no in accepting money is accepting it with a promise of a return that you know you'll be unable to keep. Often a donation will come with an off-record ask. I have heard so many requests from donors—from the obvious to the completely bonkers, and some so far out there you'd be blown away that anyone even asked in the first place. But when the money is waving in front of you, how tempting is it to say yes to absolutely anything they ask for?

During the campaign for the world-record-breaking cycling challenge that involved Prince Harry, a large bike brand agreed to a meeting with us to discuss sponsorship. They offered to provide bikes and monetary support in return for them being named as a sponsor. The pitch went great, and within a few days the marketing team came back and said they had a "provisional" yes for me for all our requirements. This would usually be a big champagne moment, but the word *provisional* had me holding back on popping the cork.

The guy went on to explain that if I could arrange a photo op of Prince Harry riding their bike the provisional would slide to a confirmed. They told me they didn't need it in the contract, but they just wanted to know I would do all I could to make it happen—a gentleman's handshake, so to speak.

Now, you may wonder why they didn't want this in the contract. This is simple—Harry on a bike would be a huge financial benefit to the company, which they'd receive with a tax write-off due to the charitable-donation element. This crosses legal guidelines, as charities cannot directly profit from donations.

I WAS NOW AT A CROSSROADS.

At this point I had all we needed for this challenge staring me in the face, and all it would have taken was a simple nod of the head for me to reach out and grab it. But at what cost? Harry was my husband's long-term friend, and they had years of trust and respect built up between them. He was not a commodity to punt around.

This was a promise I knew I could not morally or ethically keep. I knew if I said yes, I would also one day be having the conversation that I could not do what I had promised. I would be compromising my own integrity and values, and that is never worth it. You can always get another donor, but once you lower your standards and lose your value, it's incredibly hard to get it back. My advice here is to know yourself. Know your limits, know your values, and do not compromise.

This brings me nicely to the art of saying no. When you decide that your values are not aligned or are concerned about someone's legitimacy or you've decided the eighteen-page list of demands in exchange for the dollar is just too much for you to bear, you have to say no. It is always a best practice to not burn a bridge in the business of asking for money, so how do you say no without offending?

In chapter 5.3 you will learn how to be fully prepared for your ask. You will know this inside out, and you will know what you can and can't compromise on. Having this knowledge will allow you to make quick decisions. This is important, as if you have to deliver a no, you don't want to procrastinate. You know how frustrating it is to be waiting for someone to give you an answer. Being left hanging is never a good position.

If you are saying no, don't wait. Be respectful in your decline, and make sure you thank them for their time. Keep it simple and to the point. If you are saying no because you have discovered a misalignment during the conversation, or their ask is too high, resist the urge to discuss this. No matter how hard you try to dress it up, it will come across as offensive. As always, don't burn the bridge. You never know when you might speak to this person again. Imagine that they are moving to the very company that's your dream investor. Treat them like they're already there.

Building a solid professional network is never something to be sniffed at. If you are unable to give the no there and then for a legitimate reason other than fear, then give it as soon as possible after the meeting. Aim for a phone call first. Emails and texts also make it seem that they are not that important to you.

SUMMARY
HOW NOT TO RECEIVE MONEY

$ Don't show a lack of gratitude.

$ Don't accept money illegally or immorally.

$ Don't accept money from a source that does not align with your values.

$ Don't promise a return that you cannot fulfill.

$ Don't be a yes man. Know how to say no.

CHAPTER THREE

FEAR

WHAT IS FEAR?

Firstly, I want to say that I've read many a book about fear—many written by, well, shall I say "the tough guy" or the "hard man," who claims fear doesn't exist. It's all about how tough you are. Fear is something associated with weak people, and real badasses never get scared.

Well, I am here to tell you if you hear or read that anywhere, you're entitled to call bullshit! For years I've worked alongside some of the toughest, meanest badasses any nation has produced—the world's best of the best, guys who make the Expendables look like the bubble guppies. Heck, I even married one of them!

One thing I can tell you for sure about every one of them is that they *all* get scared sometimes. Every one of them feels fear. No one is immune.

So what do you think of when you think of fear? Do you go to the scary movies you saw as a child? Your biggest phobias? Exciting theme parks, loss, grief, or an anxious situation? Fear can be described in many ways, and it is defined as an unpleasant, often strong emotion caused by anticipation or awareness of danger or perceived danger.

But does an unpleasant emotion equate to a negative emotion? Fear can actually be a very healthy emotion that's warning your nervous system, your gut, to initiate your survival instincts. Fear becomes unhealthy when we allow it to take over and control our rational thinking, making it irrational and preventing us from doing things.

Fear comes in two forms. First there is **survival fear**. This occurs when there is a belief that someone or something is dangerous and likely to cause pain or harm or is a threat to you in general. It is a survival response that can trigger strong physical reactions. When fear is present, your amygdala is triggered. The amygdala is a small mass found deep in the temporal lobe that operates our fight, flight, or freeze instincts.

Public speaking, failure, rejection, and judgment are some of the most common fears people possess, and yes, all of these are involved in asking for money. Knowing you're going to be in this position can trigger these fears and kick your amygdala into action, causing the release of cortisol and adrenaline—your stress hormones, which prepare your body to fight or run.

You may start to perspire or have difficulty speaking. Your heart is racing, and you experience a cold, sweaty feeling with goosebumps all over. Needless to say, this is not the ideal physical state for standing in front of a group of investors asking for money.

How do you control this? How can you stop the release of these hormones and avoid looking like a sweaty, stuttering mess?

Think of some of your earliest childhood fears: fear of the dark, of the *thing* under the bed, the ghosts in the shadows. Anyone who has looked after a small child at some point will be familiar with the nightly activity of checking for monsters.

"NO, NOTHING IN THE CUPBOARD. NOPE, NOTHING UNDER THE BED, NOTHING BEHIND THE DOOR. I THINK THE MONSTER IS GONE, BUT DO YOU WANT ME TO LEAVE THE LIGHT ON?"

Now, I don't want to be assumptive, but I presume if you are cohabitating you've never had to do this with your other half. I'd be surprised if your partner has ever started to walk up the dark stairs before stopping and giving you the *will you walk up with me* look. That's because our imagination is our brain trying to make sense of the world, and as you grow, you learn the dark staircase is nothing to fear. Ghosts are in the movies, and monsters are not real.

Your knowledge has expanded, so your imagination begins to fade. You are no longer afraid of the boogeyman; you have come to learn he simply doesn't exist. However, the ghost in the cupboard, the dark hallway, and the monster under the bed do still exist as metaphors for your fear of the unknown. When you enter a situation where outcomes are unknown, like a job interview or a public-speaking event, you revert straight back to your five-year-old self, sitting in your pjs on the bed, terrified to look under it. The person sitting across that interview table is your unknown. He or she is your new boogeyman.

$ $ $

The second form of fear is **pleasure fear.** Go back once more to when you were a kid. Do you remember those times when you were still afraid of the dark? Your mom and dad had done all the checks and tucked you into a certified monster-free zone. Since you were settled and safe, Mom and Dad headed downstairs for a little alone time—that joyous moment of peace where they can kick back, kid-free, and watch a grown-up movie.

You were told you can't watch it, that it's for grown-ups. It's too scary, and that's why they wait for you to go to bed before they turn it on.

REMEMBER, YOU MUST STAY IN BED. DID YOU DO AS YOU WERE TOLD?

Or did you sneak down and peer between the banisters to catch a glimpse of the scary creatures onscreen? You knew it would scare you; you knew it was wrong, but you couldn't not look!

You soon shot back upstairs, realizing you had bitten off more than you could chew, and you lay in bed, filled with the fear you created for your little self until you finally fall asleep, probably to have a nightmare! Why was this scenario different from the monster under the bed?

As grown-ups we actively seek out this type of fear. *The Exorcist*, *IT*, and *The Conjuring* are all up there among the highest-grossing movies of all time. Haunted houses in the USA are a $300 million a year industry, and the amusement park market is worth $45.2 billion globally. As a nation, we spent phenomenal amounts of our hard-earned cash to be scared out of our wits on a regular basis.

The difference between survival fear and pleasure fear is that pleasure is staged. You make the choice to experience it, and you trust that those involved have followed all the safety checks. It feels less like an unknown and is something you have more control over.

The staged experience produces more dopamine than cortisol, so all the negative responses associated with survival fear are replaced with exhilaration and excitement. The difference between the two responses is simply what hormone is produced and how your body reacts to it.

So is it possible to control this, to trick your brain, to make your body respond to survival fear in the same way that it does to pleasure fear?

In this section I will show you how to tackle that monster under the bed and make him more like your roller coaster. You will discover how, with a few simple steps, you can switch your brain and its response when you are faced with

FEAR.

F for Failure

E for Embarrassment

A for Anticipation

R for Regret

Let me show you how to bring a whole new meaning to each of these stages and signs of fear, allowing you to flip the narrative on how your body responds.

3.1 FAILURE

When you plug the word *failure* into any internet search engine, almost all the responses are links or words that associate failure with being negative. You might see words and phrases like *subnormal*, *deficient*, *underperforming*, *flop*, *full breakdown*, or even *catastrophic disaster*.

Failure has long been seen as something very bad that we all want to avoid or something we should feel ashamed of. Society has created this unhealthy association with failure. While most people are still stuck trying to avoid failure like the plague, I personally love it.

SIMPLY PUT, IF YOU HAVE NEVER FAILED YOU HAVE NEVER TRULY TRIED.

If you are going to strive and reach for your goals in life—I mean *really* push yourself—then it's guaranteed you are going to fail at least once.

If you sit firmly in your comfort zone, never trying anything new and sticking to only what you know, then sure, you may get away without ever failing, but only because you never tried to become any better. Really, failing means you have stepped out of your comfort zone and tried something outside of your current ability set.

You don't quite make it, but you want it badly enough that you will try again. And you may fail again, but you will keep trying and learning and getting better and better, until one day you make it. On that day, your bravery will pay off. The failures become lessons, and those lessons turn into victories. The only time you can truly fail is when you stop trying. There is no shame in failing.

YOU LEARN, YOU ADAPT, AND YOU KEEP TRYING.

When I was nineteen years old, I was desperate to move on from my job as a traveling salesperson. I was tired of the twelve-hour days, being dropped off in random towns, and knocking on doors all day and night come wind, rain, or snow, selling people things they didn't want. Truth be told, I knew they didn't need it and would never use too.

Believe me, Scotland in the middle of winter is not a place you want to be knocking on doors asking people for money. It's cold, it's miserable, and the Scottish people can be unforgiving when you disturb their Friday-evening fish and chips! But I was paid on commission basis only, so if I wanted to eat that day and have a bed in the local guesthouse that evening, I had to make those sales.

One evening, during a particularly wild thunder and snowstorm in the middle of December, I was walking through the streets of a small town in northern Scotland. I'd just had what felt like the millionth door of the day slammed in my face, and I suddenly stopped, unable to feel my fingers or toes, ice-wet to my bones and shivering uncontrollably.

I told myself, *Enough is enough*. I was done! The next morning, fully thawed, I got up, grabbed a newspaper, and headed straight for the jobs section. I had no idea what I was looking for at the time, but I knew it had to be something where I could be warm and would have little risk of losing a digit to frostbite! Other than that, I was pretty much game for anything. I mentally scrolled down through the ads.

Counter assistant at McDonald's: *Well it would be warm, I guess?*

Nursing home assistant: *It's warm, it would be friendly, and hopefully no doors would get shut in my face. But the bed-pan changes! The people who do these job are absolute saints, but am I one of them?*

Waitress and table service at Private Eyes: *I don't think that's a detective agency; let's keep scrolling.*

As I was almost ready to give up hope and get my hat, scarf, and gloves back on, there it was.

$ **Do you have a flare for sales?**

$ **Are you comfortable working toward targets?**

$ **Are you comfortable asking people for money?**

YES, YES, I AM! I CAN DO ALL THAT!

I applied for the job immediately and was accepted for the interview. I booked my time slot and began preparations for the meeting.

Interviews had always been my strongest point. I actually enjoyed preparing and researching for them, and they were never situations that made me nervous. This goes back to my mother's words about having greater things to concern myself with.

I was always armed with at least the basics: knowing my resume, my strengths, and my weaknesses, along with at least a few interesting things about the company I was interviewing for. I breezed through all the usual questions. Then the interviewer began to look nervous. He shifted around in his chair as he prepared himself for the next question.

OH GOD, I THOUGHT TO MYSELF.

What could it be? I knew this job sounded too good to be true. What sinister thing is he about to ask me that's making him so nervous?

Then it came.

"ALANA, UMM ... HOW DO YOU FEEL ABOUT ASKING PEOPLE FOR MONEY?"

As he said the words, his eyes dropped, and he looked almost embarrassed about having asked me the question.

IS THAT ALL?

I'd been ready for this guy to tell me I would have to bury the bodies of unruly clients or something.

"I HAVE NO ISSUE WITH ASKING PEOPLE FOR MONEY," I TOLD HIM.

Suddenly his nervousness turned to a look of shock. "Really?" he said, removing his glasses.

"Sure, I actually quite enjoy it!" I replied confidently.

Just then I could see him mentally drawing a big tick on that notepad he was playing around with, and then the final question came.

"Well, Alana, this job is for a debt recovery agency, and you will be required to attend customers' homes, are you comfortable with this?"

Well, it was no different than what I was doing already—turning up unwelcomed at homes and asking people for money. And at least with this job I'd be getting paid properly for it.

"Absolutely!" I replied.

The interviewer gave me a big smile. "Well, that's perfect, Alana. I can tell you, between you and me, I think it's safe to say we will be welcoming you to our team."

I was overjoyed! I had a new job, and I'd get to keep hold of all my fingers and toes!

We discussed dates, and excitement filled me. He told me I could get started in four weeks, and then he dropped the next bombshell. "You'll receive a full salary and benefits package, and you will be given a company car. I'll just need a copy of your driving license, and that's us all set!" His eager little face smiled at me.

Oh right, yes of course—that would be the driving license I'd ticked yes to having on my application form but that I didn't actually have yet!

"Sure thing! I'll get that to you," I said with what I hoped was Oscar-worthy confidence. *OK, don't panic, Alana. You have four weeks! How hard can it be?*

Now this wasn't America where they let you slide by with an automatic car and a quick test. This was Scotland, where everyone who wants to drive has to pass a manual test and take a written exam.

I booked in for the written exam immediately, which had to be passed before I could book the driving exam. I sat and passed the academic test with no problem, which possibly gave me a false sense of security.

Things did not run so smoothly when it came to the practical driving test. I knew I could drive! I knew everything I needed to do when it came to driving, but my nerves and self-doubt when I sat with the instructor proved to be my undoing. I took the first practical driving test a week after my interview.

I FAILED.

What did I do wrong? I'm such a disappointment! What a failure! Can I even do this?

I was devastated and full of self-doubt and shame, but I'd accepted the job and still had three weeks left to get that license I needed. So I went back a few days later to sit for attempt two of my practical driving test. The instructor met me at the car, got in, and gave no conversation or eye contact. We went straight into the exam.

I FAILED AGAIN.

Oh my gosh, how useless am I? I am a huge disappointment! What an even bigger failure than I imagined! Quit now, woman!

I was very frustrated and angry with myself, but my start day for the new job was looming, so I gave myself a shake and booked in immediately for my next try at the test. With two weeks to go until I started the job, I was heading for my third attempt.

FOR A THIRD TIME I FAILED.

Jesus, you are an embarrassment to yourself and everyone who knows you! Why even bother? Just quit now!

I gave myself another shake and told myself quitting wasn't an option. I wanted this job badly! So I booked the test again. Is there such a thing as fourth-time luck? (Apparently not.)

I FAILED AGAIN!

I'd made four attempts and had four fails. I went home, and I cried—a lot. The self-doubt and self-deprecation were now in a full-blown outpour! I started questioning everything.

What's wrong with me? What's going wrong? Why can't I do this? I should give up for sure!

I sat there in full poor-me mode, and I looked up at a picture of my mom on the side table. As I stared at her eyes I thought about her short thirty-seven years of life, and this overwhelming feeling came over me. It told me to stop feeling sorry for myself and sort my shit out.

I put the self-doubt firmly aside and went into self-reflection. I stopped with the self-deprecation and moved into self-analysis. I quickly realized that as soon as I'd booked the first test, I'd put myself under a huge amount of pressure. If I didn't pass the test,

I wouldn't get the job, and I'd be back pounding the streets and freezing my ass off, getting a hundred doors a day slammed in my face. I continued taking that same mindset into each progressive test. I wasn't learning; I wasn't adapting; I was just doing the same thing over and over again and hoping for a different result—the very definition of insanity!

I once again gave myself a shake, but this time I was going to attack this differently. I began to analyze the test days. What had they looked like each time? I'd get to the site and wait in the yard, where I'd get extremely nervous, my adrenaline pumping. Then I would meet the instructor and attempt some small talk, only to receive no response. I was outwardly anxious, convinced that I would mess up. My mind was on everything I didn't know, trying to remember everything I had learned about becoming a driver.

I was behaving like a learner. I wasn't going there to become a learner, so why was I behaving like one? I wanted the instructor to see me as an accomplished driver, but I was displaying every sign of being a nervous student. I got it. It was all within my own head and all within my own control. I went straight to booking my fifth test. I asked a friend if I could borrow her car and asked if she could come along with me. (Obviously she had plates on and was a licensed driver.)

The morning of the test arrived, and I got straight into character. I was no longer a student; I was an experienced driver heading out for a drive with a friend. I got into the car and offered her a lift. We drove to the test center and just chatted about the normal things friends on a drive chat about. I pulled up and waited for my instructor, and when she appeared, I walked up to her, looked her straight in the eye, reached out my hand, and gave her a firm, confident handshake. We headed to the car. I wasn't taking a test, I was taking her for a drive.

My energy was the complete opposite of every other time, and it was clear to me things were already different when the instructor responded to my attempted small talk. We got into a conversation, and she told me all about herself and even began to open up to me about her recent cancer treatment. It was then I knew I had finally passed the awkward driving lesson experience. We were now getting more personal, which was exactly what I needed.

This was also an age-old technique in the practice of being a salesperson and getting a sale—getting your client to open up and tell you close, personal things—the more intimate the better. It tells you there is now trust. I knew I was in.

The forty minutes flew by. We pulled the car back into the parking lot, and before we even took off our seatbelts, she turned to me and said those words I'd waited so long to hear:

"YOU PASSED!"

I had passed! The instructor seemed even more excited about it than I was. I was elated and couldn't help but inappropriately hug her. We said our goodbyes, she handed me my pass certificate, and I started preparing for my new job, which was due to commence the following Monday. I sent in all the paperwork and was just lucky they never checked the date!

I HAD SWITCHED FAILURE TO FORTUNE.

If I had excepted failure, if I had not kept trying, and if I had just given up, I would never have been able to achieve what I desired. It was not about the failures, but what

I was learning, how I was adapting, and how I was growing.

The only time I see it as acceptable for someone to say they failed is if they never tried—if they allowed the fear of failure to matter more to them than the achievement itself. Failure will always be a part of the journey to success, and the only time you ever truly fail is when you never start in the first place. Use your failures. Turn them into positive experiences, learn your lessons, and continue to always grow.

SWITCH FAILURE TO FORTUNE.

3.2 EMBARRASSMENT

When most people imagine themselves asking for money, they envision themselves in a scene from *Oliver!*, like they are approaching Mr. Bumble in their orphan rags with their bowl extended, looking up and saying needily,

"PLEASE, SIR, CAN I HAVE SOME MORE?"

If you haven't had the experience of witnessing Lionel Bart's masterpiece, another vivid image would be sitting on a cardboard box on the sidewalk whispering, "Please, mister, can you spare some change?"

What I'm saying is that, for many people, asking for money is a terrifying and humiliating experience. They feel they are degrading themselves and that this experience is something to be ashamed of.

Is asking for money something to be ashamed of? Well, from my experience, I can say without much of a doubt that since developing these methods, I have never experienced any guilt or shame when it comes to asking for money. Why? Because not only am I fully comfortable with my own worth, but I am also always fully confident in my ask, my reasons for my ask, the mutual benefits of my ask, and the full details of the relationship being discussed.

I am ready, I am prepared, and I know exactly what I am doing when I enter the room.

I'M LIKE THIS NOW, BUT IT WASN'T ALWAYS LIKE THAT.

Back in my twenties, when I was a young debt collector, the one thing I hated the most about my job was repossessing cars. When you are in the world of recovery, most would say that when there are possessions and assets such as homes, cars, or valuable collections that it is much easier to work the debt collection because if you can't make them pay, you can always take the asset and send it to an auction to recover some cash.

A great majority of debt collectors, and I hate to say it but mostly the male debt collectors, thrived on the thrill of the chase, getting the payment at any cost to satisfy their egos. However, for me, this was not my main purpose in debt collecting.

I had grown up in that family environment. My mother and I had hidden behind the door as the collections guy banged it down. I never wanted others to feel that fear. I always wanted to find a solution, first and foremost, that could help them find a way out of the giant hole they found themselves in. That was my main objective. I wasn't there to exasperate the issue; I wanted to make it better.

As an example, let's look at repossessing a person's work van. Let's say the debt is ten thousand dollars. You repossess the van and get maybe five thousand for it at auction—if you are lucky. There's still a five thousand dollar debt, and on top of that they now have legal bills, tow fees, my fees, auction fees, and to top it all off, you have taken away their only means of actually earning an income.

How are they meant to be able to get this debt paid if you have removed their only means of transportation? You've now taken this situation from a difficult scenario to a seemingly impossible one. This is one of the reasons I found repossession a terrible solution to debt, but it wasn't the only reason—and it wasn't the reason I found it so difficult and uncomfortable.

No, the real reason I avoided property re-possessions like the plague was that I wasn't actually very good at it. I didn't really know what I was doing, and no one had ever actually taught me how to do it properly. I got flustered, and my adrenaline would pump every time I saw it on my task list. I hated it, and trying to work out how to do it was akin to Homer Simpson taking a Mensa exam—just pointless! Therefore, I would do everything in my power to avoid opening a repossession case. Those files always made their way to the bottom of the pile.

$ $ $

In 2008 I was working at a financial institution. If you're familiar with the financial sector, then you know that 2008 was not a great time to be in banking. The global financial crisis—the most serious financial crisis since the Great Depression—had hit, and foreclosures, bankruptcies, and repossessions were at an all-time high. The powers-that-be in the bank were not messing about, and they demanded immediate action on any defaults.

I knew there was no longer any way to avoid my great unknown. I knew repossessions would become part of my everyday work life now, so I had the choice to either quit or educate myself. All it took was the memory of my old job pounding the cold, wet, miserable streets of Scotland to know that quitting wasn't something I was willing to do. That left me only one option: I had to adapt and learn.

I studied every available piece of educational material on asset recovery on the online catalogue of courses at my workplace. I committed to memory all the ins and outs of the process—the full rundown. I studied and soaked it all in.

When work was finished for the day, I went home and kept learning. I learned during the weekends and on my days off. I grew more and more knowledge, and as fast as my knowledge grew, my fear subsided at the same rate. Before too long I was able to say that I not only understood the process of repossession, but was also fully capable of putting into action every step from start to finish. My fear was gone, my nerves were gone, and my great unknown was gone.

I had avoided asset recoveries for so long, and the longer my avoidance had gone on, the more embarrassed I'd become when it came to asking for help with how to do them. Once I got through that and actually educated myself on the process I'd been avoiding, the embarrassment factor disappeared, the anxiety went away, and I no longer worried about doing them.

Don't get me wrong—it still wasn't a pleasant part of my job. I did not feel happy about performing repossessions, but having the full knowledge of what I was doing made the process a lot easier—not just for me, but also for the client experiencing the repossession. Since I had become fully capable and free from my fear of what I didn't know, I could focus my energy on determining the best solutions for my clients. I could give them the focus and attention they needed.

$ $ $

Knowledge and education are not the only tools one can use to get over insecurity, and embarrassment can come in many forms.

I was badly burned in an accident when I was a young girl, and I was heavily scarred over much of my upper body. My arms and chest bore the most visible scarring. My first taste of real humiliation came on my first trip to the local swimming pool after the accident.

Before the accident I had been a total water baby. I'd been a regular at the pool and had taken many classes. I loved swimming and had missed it badly since the accident.

I was super excited as my friends and I headed off to the pool. I was excited, though a little self-conscious, to slip into my bathing suit and get back into the water.

My friends and I all quickly got changed in the locker room and headed straight to the pool. One by one, my friends jumped in, but just as I was about to follow them in, the lifeguard blew his whistle. I looked around to see what had happened and was surprised to see him looking at me and motioning for me to come speak to him.

As I approached, I could see him looking at my scars with obvious disgust on his face. I got it. They were by no means pleasant to look at, as I knew myself from seeing them in the mirror. He continued staring as he told me I could not enter the pool. He told me he was concerned about open wounds—despite them being completely healed—and that I would have to put a T-shirt on as I might also frighten some of the younger children. He let me know I wouldn't be allowed in the pool unless I covered up.

I WAS ONLY NINE YEARS OLD.

I went back to the changing room feeling incredibly low. I just wanted to go home. But my friends were waiting for me, so I grabbed my black-and-white T-shirt, pulled it on over my suit, and headed back to the pool. Only now I felt as though everyone was looking at me for being in the pool with my clothes on.

My humiliation was on overload. I stayed for a short while, but the first opportunity I got to escape, I was out of there. After that, I avoided swimming at all costs. I made every excuse under the sun at school to skip swimming classes, and I stopped going with my friends to the pool. The joy I'd once felt in the water had turned to shame.

When I met my husband, he was this incredible adventurous Special Forces guy with the nickname *The Frogman*. With a name like that, it was no surprise that water was a huge part of his life. He loved everything about water: surfing, swimming, diving. Anything associated with getting wet subsurface, and he was in his happy place.

I watched over the years while he jumped in the pool with the kids. I watched while he took on the distances length by length. I watched while he was the first one down the water slides, and I watched while he got excited when there were any water-sport activities on the menu on holidays.

I WATCHED.

It wasn't that the thought of water still filled me with dread, no. The truth was I loved everything about water. The sea to me is one of the most beautiful, magical places there is. No, the problem was I allowed the shame that lifeguard had bestowed on me to deprive me of that joy for many, many years.

Now I worried about jumping in as I feared I lacked the muscle memory of being in the water. When you work out your body, you gain fitness and muscle. Over the years you may gain or lose your level of shape and fitness, but your body has a way of remembering. It's a lot easier to get back to a level you once had than to try to achieve something you never had before, later on in life.

OUR MINDS WORK IN THE EXACT SAME WAY.

A good way to explain this is when you hear people say, "It's like riding a bike."

WHAT THAT MEANS IS YOUR MIND REMEMBERS.

It may have been years since you rode that bike, but as soon as you sit in the saddle your mind remembers, and before long you are peddling away.

Whether its mind or body, when you start working out that muscle it reminds you that you've done it before, and it's not that hard. You were capable once, so you can be capable now. But for me, jumping in the water, going down the slide, racing underwater, and all these things—I had either lost my childhood muscle memory, or I had just never gained it at all. Because my subconscious wasn't reminding me that I could do it, whenever I thought of trying, I was filled with anxiousness and fear of embarrassment that something may go wrong, that the lifeguard may once again blow his whistle.

One day, however, I thought of my own beliefs about failure and my mom's words about the opinions of ignorance. I realized the fear of embarrassment and that lifeguard's words had been holding me back from truly enjoying my life. I was missing giggles from the kids, happy memories, and exhilaration—all due to this fear.

SO WHAT IF I COULD TURN THAT ANTICIPATED FEELING OF FEAR OF EMBARRASSMENT INTO A FEELING OF PURE EXCITEMENT AND ENJOYMENT?

WHAT IF I DIDN'T ALLOW THE NEGATIVE INTRUSIVE THOUGHTS TO HOLD ME BACK?

WHAT IF JUST LET GO AND JUMPED IN?

That is exactly what I did. It was a beautiful sunny day, and I was on vacation with my family. The kids were laughing and screaming as my husband threw them into the pool, one after the other. He was getting the better of them, like he always did, and I was sitting by the edge watching them all having fun. Something suddenly just switched in my mind.

I STOOD UP AND TOOK OFF MY COVER-UP, AND AS SOON AS I JUMPED IN THE POOL ALL THOSE FEELINGS OF FEAR DISAPPEARED,

immediately replaced with exhilaration, excitement, and laughter. The kids were over the moon—so excited to have Mommy in the pool and to have me on their team to take down Daddy!

Now I have that mantra in my head whenever I feel that fear of embarrassment enter my mind. I know that is the exact moment when I need to do it, whatever it is. Now I never say no to anything that the kids ask me to do if my reason for saying no is born from fear of embarrassment. Now I jump in the pool, dive into the soft play drop, jump out of planes, you name it. As long there is a low chance of death or major bodily harm, I am doing it!

I want you to understand how important it is to overcome your own fear of embarrassment, because when I speak with people about what is holding them back when asking for money, one of the most common responses I get is,

"I DON'T WANT TO LOOK STUPID!"

The mere anticipation of the fear of embarrassment, the thought of being turned down, or the idea that they may look silly overtakes everything else, including the thought of what might happen if they get a yes. The avoidance of embarrassment is enough to stop many people taking that next step to getting what they actually want. They walk away from what they dream of because of the shame they have created in their own head, without it actually occurring.

You must switch your mindset to no longer accept that anxious feeling, that nervousness of being humiliated, and that belief that you will look silly, into one that is focused on the prize. Focus on the feeling of exhilaration you'll get when they say yes, the joy you'll feel when you receive it, and the adventures you will have putting the money to the uses you have planned for it. All those feeling should always, always trump embarrassment.

SWITCH EMBARRASSMENT TO EXCITEMENT.

3.3 ANTICIPATION
"ANTICIPATION IS WORSE THAN PARTICIPATION."

We often psych ourselves out of a situation before having any knowledge of what is coming. We practice a doomsday mindset by thinking of everything that could go wrong. We're consumed by nerves over what a person will say. We get that overproduction of adrenaline and cortisol, our palms are sweaty, our hearts are pumping, and our mouths are so dry we have no idea how the pitch words can ever pass through the sand desert it has become. We spend so much time anticipating what might be that participation in the actual event becomes our worst nightmare.

Think about a first date with that guy or girl you have been excited about asking out or even one you swiped right, (Is that the right direction? I have no idea.) and you couldn't believe they agreed to a date. You spend the evening selecting the perfect outfit, making sure your look is on point, thinking of some funny and quirky anecdotes, and perfecting the right level of sexiness and coyness.

Yes, that goes for ladies and gents; we all do the pre-act rehearsals. We think of everything that could possibly go wrong, from our own acts to who they might be.

Will you walk in and fall flat on your face? Blurt out an inappropriate joke? Get food stuck in your teeth? Or will they talk endlessly about their ex who they are most definitely not over yet? Maybe show an inherent rudeness to every person who serves you over the course of the evening?

You think of every possible thing that might go wrong with this date and only very occasionally of something that might go right. Either way, you are all about the anticipation. The fear associated with anticipation can often overwhelm people so much they don't go ahead with the plan; they cancel the date, the skydive, or the job interview, all over fear of what might happen.

The thing is the participation is very rarely the same as the anticipation. Falling flat on your face on the way to the table will probably never happen, and even if it did, would it really be the end of the world? Or would it provide a hilarious ice breaker and start the evening with a story to tell the grandkids if everything works out well? Would the feeling of achieving that adrenaline buzz from jumping out of a plane outweigh the fear of anticipation? How much would getting that job change your life over never knowing? A life spent giving into the fear of anticipation will lead to a life of regrets and what-ifs.

Now, I am by no means playing down anticipation anxiety. It is a very real thing. What I am saying is that it can be managed, controlled, and beaten.

The first task is to make sure you are in the best possible position to deal with it. This is a mind, body, and soul job. If you are spending your days in bed eating ice cream and cookies, worrying about what-ifs and feeling anxiety build up more and more, you are giving in. All those daily bad habits are contributing to your fear.

Poor diet and lack of exercise are two of the biggest contributing factors to anxiety. Going into a pitch after a heavy night of food and alcohol, full of fear and body shakes, well you just wouldn't do it, or at least I hope you wouldn't.

WHY NOT?

We all know a heavy night of partying will lead to poor sleep, jitters, and a very nervously delivered pitch. This outcome will be the same if you go in without having exercised, full of junk food and E numbers. If your pitch is coming up in the next week, give yourself the seven days to take regular walks outside, eat healthily, get sun and fresh air, and generally get your mind, body, and soul into the right place. This isn't a diet book, so I won't go too deeply into this. But even just the basics will help you.

The next task is to practice by talking to other people. Most of the time the anxiousness can be talked out with a friend. Being too much in your own head can overwhelm you and you can overdramatize every aspect of the situation. When you talk to an outsider, someone who is impartial to the situation, you will soon realize what you feel is a big deal is really nothing at all.

Finally, find a way to ground yourself. This can be done with yoga, meditation, or even snapping rubber bands on your wrists. There are many ways to do this, and you can even invent your own. It's about finding a distraction—something that will deter your thoughts away from the anxiousness.

Remember that this is an opportunity, something to be cherished and relished. Appreciate the chance you have been given. If your nerves are coming out as anticipation, switch them to appreciation. You are lucky to be in this position, and perhaps many others would love to be exactly where you are. Gratitude can go a long way to eliminating the nerves associated with anticipation.

SWITCH ANTICIPATION TO APPRECIATION.

3.4 REGRET

Remember that moment when you are finally ready to go for it. You've finally plucked up the courage to ask the girl you've crushed on since fourth grade out on a date. You have practiced what you will say and make your move toward her, looking and feeling as cool as you can. She makes eye contact; this is it.

She smiles at you. The smile turns coy, then into a smirk, and suddenly, before you can make a sound, she says, "Dude, not a chance."

You are immediately consumed with the most overwhelming feeling. You are in panic mode about the recourse, and of course, filled with regret. She said no. You have been rejected. What happens now?

HOW WILL I EVER LOOK THEM IN THE EYES AGAIN?

HOW WILL THEY BE AFTERWARD?

That feeling of rejection will remain with you through your childhood and early adulthood, and if left unresolved it will remain part of your character for life. It will stay in every relationship you have and will form part of every negotiation, whether work or personal, that will ever take place in your life. The fear of rejection, regret, and recourse will pump through your veins for as long as you allow it.

Most people live with regret and will often dwell on those bad moments throughout their lives. How one handles situations and disappointments is often defined by early childhood experiences. So what happens to those who had it easy? Those who were the stars of the school, the ones who were never knocked back, those who most likely never had to ask for anything because it always came to them?

One would assume those who have an easy ride won't have any regrets and will sail through life, right?

In fact, it's quite the opposite.

Those who experience hardship, who learn at the school of hard knocks, and who get early childhood lessons in resilience have all kinds of experience dealing with regret. On the other hand, those with easy rides in childhood often grow up with very little resilience. When rejection comes later in life, which inevitably happens to us all, they will have no muscle memory for resilience and may handle situations like this very badly. They won't have built up any tools in their armory to use in situations outside of their comfort zones.

When I was fifteen, just after I'd lost my mum to cancer, I told myself I would have no regrets in life. My mum was thirty-seven years old when she died. She lived her life in service to other people. She looked after her sisters, mother, and father and then married on her eighteenth birthday. She had children soon after, then got divorced at thirty and raised three kids on her own.

She was diagnosed with cancer at thirty-six and died at thirty-seven. I knew there was an incredible amount of regret there. She died not knowing what would happen to her six-, fifteen- and seventeen-year-old children. She knew her dreams of having a thriving business, being in love, and raising grandchildren would never transpire. She was a beautiful woman who was incredibly strong and driven, but cancer does not discriminate. It took her life at thirty-seven years old, while I watched on at fifteen.

And that was when I developed a life mantra I live by every day.

I WOULD RATHER REGRET THE THINGS I HAVE DONE THAN REGRET THE THINGS I NEVER HAD THE COURAGE TO DO.

I have lived by this my entire life, and it is something that has never failed me, even if in the moment I feel different. If I mess up, if I don't achieve my goal, and if I make a total fool of myself, one thing will always be true: at least I gave it a go. I tried, and whether I succeeded or not, I most definitely got further than the guy who was too proud to even give it a shot.

When it comes to decision-making, life can either be full of what-ifs, regrets, or achievements. Obviously, achievements are amazing, but when it comes to what-ifs or regrets, I have very rarely heard of a regret that is not full of lessons, anecdotes, and future avoidance techniques. Some regrets are filled with pain and disappointments and cannot be altered. You may wish some things had never happened, but even these regrets will give you lessons and make you stronger for future endeavors.

I vividly remember my mother sitting in Roxburghe House in Aberdeen, Scotland, an end-of-life respite where she spent her final days. A couple of days before her departure, I visited her. We sat together but said very little. She was on very high doses of morphine and barely able to speak.

We stared out of the window at a red squirrel who would often appear to say hello. I was fifteen years old, and instead of thinking of the last remaining moments I should be savoring with my mom, I was thinking about the guy I was dating and the party I'd be attending that evening.

The morphine had rendered her fairly mute, so my mind was free to wander. But then, this sunny spring Thursday afternoon, she took hold of my hand and said, "Ice cream."

I looked right into her eyes, her face gaunt. She was nothing like the voluptuous blonde she'd been just six months prior. She was barely eighty pounds and resembled a ninety-year-old more than a woman in her thirties.

"Ice cream?" I repeated. She looked at me with every effort of an Olympian preparing for going for gold and nodded her head.

I jumped up straight away. I couldn't remember the last time she had eaten. I headed straight out of the room and on the hunt for ice cream like a contestant of the Hunger Games. I found a nurse who pointed me in the direction of the canteen.

I suddenly stopped in my tracks. I recognized my mom's doctor, and he was walking quickly toward me.

"I need to talk to you," he said.

I looked toward the canteen and back at him. I knew by the look on his face he had something important to say.

"What's up?" I asked, my tone hurried and agitated.

He asked if I were there alone, and I told him I was. By this point I was getting impatient.

"We have your mum's works back. I am afraid it's not good news," he said methodically.

At fifteen I knew what this meant to an extent; however, it was hard to understand. He proceeded to tell me it was now a matter of hours, maybe days if we were lucky. There was nothing more they could do. Up to this point my internal optimist had believed it wasn't real, that she would be fine, that she was coming home soon.

His words sunk in, and I knew it would be over soon. It was too much to take. I wandered out of the hospital. Leaving the grounds in a total daze.

I didn't want to see this. I didn't want to know this. I left the grounds of the hospital and went home. I had wandered off, mind and body, wanting to avoid everything I'd heard.

Two days later I got a message to say my mom had died.

Emptiness filled me, but that was soon replaced with an enormous sense of regret. *The ice cream!*

I NEVER BROUGHT HER THE ICE CREAM!

It was all she had wanted, the only thing she had asked me for, and I let her down. What happened? Why did I forget, and how could I do that? What kind of daughter was I? What kind of person was I?

That feeling of deep regret and self-loathing stayed with me for a long time. It was a feeling I never wanted to experience again. This is when I formed my mantra of *no regrets*. I know now what happened and why my young self dealt with the traumatic situation the way I did, but to this day the memory has remained with me. It has also remained my only regret for a thing I didn't do.

Sure, I have made many mistakes and have many regrets about things I *did* do, but those I can deal with, as at least I tried and learned for the future. Not bringing that ice cream to my mom was the one and only regret for something that I didn't do and will remain the only *what-if* I'll ever have to live with.

Whether the regret is over something you did or didn't do, you are 100 percent in control of it—both how it's handled and how it's executed. Accountability and responsibility play key roles here, and while my advice of always giving it a go remains firm, I also say that when it comes to your actions, the buck should always stop with you.

It is a natural self-preserving action to try and blame someone else when you mess up; however, this level of mindset only prolongs the lessons that are there to be learned. Taking responsibility from the offset will save you a whole lot of time. I don't have any regrets for what I didn't do other than that ice cream, and I can't change that.

The regrets for what I *have* done, however, have filled me with embarrassment, failure, letdowns, lessons, and painful thoughts. For every regret I have, one thing is most definitely true: I have gained more for each and every experience than I have lost, and I have always been accountable for my own actions. Every regret has filled me with more experiences, more knowledge, and more growth. This is how you turn regret into reward.

In life, worrying about regret, recourse, and remorse will get you nowhere. Think about what you have gained from the experience and turn the fear of regret into the excitement of the reward.

SWITCH REGRET TO REWARD.

SUMMARY

$ **Switching the Fear**

$ **Failure to Fortune**

$ **Embarrassment to Excitement**

$ **Anticipation to Appreciation**

$ **Regret to Reward**

"You gain **STRENGTH, COURAGE,** and **CONFIDENCE** by every experience in which you really **STOP TO LOOK FEAR IN THE FACE**. *You must do the thing you think you cannot do.*"

—Eleanor Roosevelt

PART TWO

MAPS—ASK AND RECEIVE

CHAPTER FOUR

INTRODUCTION TO MAPS

So far you have learned how to identify motivation factors, how not to ask for money, and hopefully you have gained a better understanding of your fear and how to channel it. You are now ready to start the process of perfecting the art of asking for money. If my years of fundraising and asking for money had to be summarized into one sentence it would be:

FAILURE TO PREPARE IS PREPARING TO FAIL.

The most common questions I'm asked that prompted me to write this book are:

$ **How do I ask for money?**

$ **What is your secret to raising so much money?**

$ **Do you get nervous when you ask for money?**

I would sometimes find it very difficult to summarize into simple terms, and that is when I came up with the MAPS formula. The truth was, asking for money seemed so easy to me. I didn't find it difficult; in fact, I found it simple and never got nervous doing it. I practiced the same method time and time again, and it really never fails when done correctly.

It isn't magic and doesn't take a PhD, but it does take work. If you think you can make it work by simply walking into the room unprepared, lacking in knowledge and relying on your good luck and charm, then I would say you should start preparing for failure. I have said failure is just a stepping stone to success, but some failures you need not endure.

USING THE MAPS FORMULA, YOU WILL ALWAYS BE READY.

Why MAPS?

The first map is believed to have been invented by Greek academic Anaximander in the sixth century. Maps were invented to develop knowledge of time and space.

They gave people direction and showed a steady path to journeymen. They are there to help you move from one place to another, to keep you organized and help you get where you want to be.

Over time maps have developed with modern technology to include GPS and Android Maps and include features like avoiding traffic, hazards, and roadblocks. This has given modern humans a more convenient and swift method of traveling.

Much like the evolution of maps of the world, my formula for fundraising has adapted over time and evolved with each new lesson I have learned. With each adaptation the basics have always remained the same.

In order to create a foolproof fundraising campaign, the process needs to be managed effectively and efficiently. This includes having:

$ the right **mindset,**

$ being **accountable** for your actions,

$ correct **planning,** and

$ implementing the **strategy.**

The following four chapters break down each of these four areas in full and will show you how to put the full MAPS plan into practice.

CHAPTER FIVE

MINDSET

In order to step into the boardroom, office, call or video chat, whatever space you are entering, the first key element is to be completely in the right mindset. The mindset you adapt with pitching to an investor or donor should be approached much like the mindset of an actor completing an audition or a reality television singing contest auditionee stepping onto the X.

The auditions that always entertain everyone, keep everyone interested and tuned in are the ones that are flawed, that are funny, that are just downright awful, or every now and then, out of this world, mind-blowingly amazing—but I'm sure if you asked Simon Cowell, he would tell you the latter are few and far between. The funny, flawed, and awful ones are the ones that fill the most airtime and keep everyone tuning in.

The psychology behind this and the reason viewers can't get enough are associated with the pleasure human minds derive when watching others make complete fools of themselves. It gives people a feeling of "I'm not the only one."

We tune in and keep watching every week to see these people; however, the ones who really last, the ones who stick with us and make us go out and buy records or download tracks in the millions, are the ones like Carrie Underwood, Kelly Clarkson, and Ruben Studdard. What carried these singers to success over everyone else?

Simple.

THEY UNDERSTOOD THE ASSIGNMENT.

In 2002 Kelly Clarkson entered that room to audition for *American Idol* and just took over that room. She was in control of the set, even sitting on a judge's chair. She was prepared, not only practically for the audition, but also her mindset was firmly in the right place. She went in there as a winner. She acted like the winner, projected like a winner, and believed she was the winner. Your pitch should be delivered in the exact same manner.

Nerves, self-doubt, anxiety, and impostor syndrome all contribute to a poor presentation, but only when they aren't addressed and you walk them into the room with you. You see, even the cockiest, most confident egomaniac has moments of doubt and anxiety. No one is immune.

Only when we don't work on our weaknesses and accept all these things as givens do most fall down, often to afraid to get back up to retry. Nerves are, of course, a natural occurrence, and without exception we all experience them. They are, however, simply your body's stress response to any given situation. In order to control your nerves so that they work for you and not against you during the process of asking for money, here are my top two tips:

1. **Know your pitch.**
2. **Know your mind.**

I will go further into knowing your pitch later, but how do you really know your mind?

If I asked you while you were sober to do the pitch when you are intoxicated, you would tell

89

me I am crazy. However, if I asked you *while* you were intoxicated to present the pitch, then that logical, sober brain would go out the window and it's likely your response would be, "Hell yeah! Let's do it!"

Unfortunately, this follows the same theory as intoxicated karaoke—good idea at the time, but the morning after it's a source of deep-rooted cringe.

When we are intoxicated, our brains release a flood of dopamine. This is your personal supply of a feel-good drink; it gives you power and confidence. Unfortunately, alcohol also impairs the part of the brain associated with good judgment, meaning you think you sound like Mariah Carey even if you actually sounds more like the systematic torture of small cats.

So how do you get confidence without the impaired judgement? This is all part of the optimum mindset formula. The amount of time spent on this for a specific event should be in direct correlation with how badly you want it. If you are trying to obtain a six-pack and biceps that would shame Arnold, going to the gym once a month and making Burger King a staple of your diet won't cut it.

If the god bod is what you really want, then it requires work and dedication. It requires dedicated time in the gym, three to six days a week, a specific and challenging plan, and a diet that supports your aims. It is the people who commit, put in the time, and stay consistent in their progress that will achieve their goals. The mind muscle works in exactly the same way. Those who are committed and dedicated are those who will develop the mindset required to knock that pitch out of the park.

How do we achieve optimum mindset?

Follow the memes!

MEMES

It's all about MEMESSS … No, not a social media funny about crazy cats or a depressed Pablo Escobar, but the seven steps to creating the optimum mindset required to have the confidence to ask for money.

$ **Meditation**

$ **Eating well**

$ **Music**

$ **Exercise**

$ **Sleep/Sun/Screen time**

Following these steps will help everyone reach the perfect state of mind to be focused, prepared, and ready for the pitch. Each step is beneficial on its own; however, the more steps you use in combination, the more powerful and controlled you will become.

Utilizing **MEMES** to achieve optimum mindset is not only beneficial to you when asking for money, but can also translate into utilization in everyday life. Optimizing your mindset on a daily basis will very quickly have a waterfall effect in all aspects of your life.

All of a sudden big problems won't seem so big, and all those little jobs you have been putting off will in time seem so easy to master. When you perfect your mindset, the only thing you will regret is not doing it sooner.

Let's look at each of these steps in more detail.

5.1 MEDITATION

There are many different forms and techniques used for meditation. Many people have spent their whole lives practicing, testing, and finding the perfect methods or optimum states to achieve perfect meditation. But what does it mean to meditate? In a nutshell, meditation is a way to push your brainwaves to operate in a state of deep relaxation.

The five most common waves that we operate in are **alpha, beta, delta, gamma,** and **theta.** In normal waking states, beta is the most common brainwave we operate in. Our beta wave is active when we are awake in normal alert consciousness. It is activated in cases of problem solving and allows us to engage in situations.

The second most common state for us to be in is delta. Delta is our sleep state, a deep sleep where our brain waves are operating at 1-4 Hz in comparison to beta that operates from 12-38 Hz. The fastest brainwaves are the gamma waves. These are active when we are in an intense state of learning and problem solving. They are associated with high levels of focus and concentration and are often active in people with high IQ.

When you meditate, your brainwaves are operating between the alpha and theta states. Some may argue that alpha state is the optimum state for meditation, as in this state you are relaxed, calm, and peaceful. You are relaxed and recharging, but you are not daydreaming.

It is said the ancient Japanese samurai were able to switch from beta to alpha instantly and were able to achieve this state of mind as a way to balance themselves during intense times of war. Personally, I enjoy the alpha state by way of a more regular meditation as you can control the moment, whether it's a few seconds or twenty minutes. It's your moment to rebalance and draw attention to your whole self. Then once you are reconnected, you can carry on with your task. The theta wave frequency is lower than the alpha state and is associated with a deep sense of relaxation, daydreaming, and an almost sleep state.

Now, what does all this have to do with asking for money? Well, the more you train your brain, the better equipped you'll be able to place yourself in the optimum state required for any given situation. When you enter the room to begin your pitch you want to ensure you are focused, calm, and balanced in order to control any unwanted hormone production, which as we know, creates nerves and anxiety when out of control.

So, going back to the samurai, how have they managed to hold their position as the toughest and most respected warriors of all time? Simply put, it is because they were trained. They trained not only their bodies, but also their minds, and they did this relentlessly and consistently. The samurai fully understood the importance of mind, body, and spirit balance.

Over years of study by many historians and experts, one thing is agreed by everyone: the Samurai's most powerful skill was their ability to stay calm under any circumstances. They were able to switch into an alpha wave in a split second through their endless training in the art of keeping calm. Once you achieve your own samurai state, you will never again walk into a room in a state of fear or nervousness.

Meditation is one of the key steps to achieving optimum mindset. It is a practice that can take thirty seconds or thirty minutes. It is all about what works for you and what makes you feel most comfortable. Enjoy experimenting and trying all the different methods that are out there, but ultimately what you want is to feel that you are in total control of your mind.

5.2 EAT WELL

When it comes to our state of mind, one of the key contributing factors to how we feel on the outside is what we put inside our bodies. Your body is a machine, and it needs to be fueled correctly to function at your optimum state. It is easy to understand what this means when it comes to physical appearance. If your daily diet consists of drive-thru, sugar highs, and mood-boosting margaritas then it is unlikely you are competing for a fitness competition, but what does this mean when it comes to our mental health?

If you have ever experienced a detox or cleansing plan you will be aware of the steps. When you pay attention to a detox you can quickly see what your body is addicted to and what is harming it.

On day one of any cleanse, you are raring to go. You are super excited and ready for the changes you know are needed. By day two you are starting to question your motives, and the excuses to quit start to creep in. Day three is the day most people quit, as the body is now in a full withdrawal stage. It is craving the drug you've been depriving it of for the last three days. Whether that drug is sugar, alcohol, caffeine, or something else, we all generally have levels of addiction to something.

The reason most people quit at day three is because their brain is telling them that this is crazy. *Why are you doing this to yourself? Just have the candy bar, and it will make everything better.* This is your conscious mind. If that mind has never completed a full detox, it is not aware what is to come. It is not aware of how good you're about to feel if you pass this stage.

If you can channel your mind to know what is ahead of you, this phase of detox becomes so much easier. When you fight the withdrawal cravings and allow your body to accept the healthy fuel you are now giving it, by day four your symptoms should start to fade, and you will now be feeling a newfound energy and zest for life.

When you fuel your body with sugar, caffeine, and soda, and your go-to stress relief are ice cream and alcohol, your body is functioning on temporary highs. I won't delve fully into the science of it all, but what I will confirm is a diet heavy in processed foods, sugars, and alcohol will most certainly give your mind a good supply of self-doubt, anxiety, tension, stress, and depression. This is because diets heavy in processed food and refined sugars lead to inflammation and impaired brain function.

Sure, it feels great in the moment, but just like drug addiction, that initial euphoric feeling doesn't last, and in order to keep up the high you need to keep topping it up, trying to get that initial buzz back. Just like any drug user will tell you, you are chasing a high that you will never catch. Instead, you end up in a prolonged high and the longer the high, the worse the low.

What goes up must come down, and when you go too high, the crash can be painful. This is where we get mood swings, anxiety, anger, and depression. To balance your mind, it is imperative to balance your nutrition. A good healthy balanced diet will keep your hormones and adrenal glands in a nice even zone where you can handle stress and high-pressure situations so much better.

I explain the detox process because the last thing you want to do is suddenly decide two days before the presentation to hit the detox.

You do not want to be heading into the presentation on day two, tired, full of excuses and headaches, and thinking of nothing else but your next glass of Malbec or bag of candy. Preparation should begin as early as possible when the big ask is coming, and a minimum of seven days would be advised.

On the run up to a presentation, you want your diet to consist of lots of good fats and proteins. The amino acids in protein help produce your own natural feel-good drugs and optimum brain function. Carbohydrates are also your friends when you select the right ones.

Complex carbohydrates such as sweet potatoes, brown rice, and starchy vegetables will all help improve your state of mind, while simple carbohydrates such as cakes, candy, and sugary cereals will give you an instant high followed by crashing lows.

Omega-3 is a key component to brain function. A diet rich in omega-3 will give you a good, strong memory and a balanced mood. Fish is a great source of omega-3. Select cold water fatty fish such as sardines, salmon, and tuna. Eggs and nuts are also excellent sources.

Iron is an important mineral for optimum body function. Sufficient iron levels are required to keep oxygen flowing steadily throughout your body. One of the first effects on the body when you have a deficiency in iron is lack of brain function. Lack of energy, brain fog, dizziness, and weakness can also occur. Foods such as liver, lean red meats, and leafy greens like spinach are perfect foods for keeping your iron intake at a good level.

Other nutrients such as **folic acid, B12,** and **thiamine** are also incredibly important for brain function.

While a diet rich in leafy greens, complex carbohydrates, lean iron-rich meats, and healthy fats and proteins will give you a significant improvement in brain health, you may also find it helpful to use natural supplements to support optimum function. Make sure you do your research when selecting these. There are many out there!

A very simple way to optimize your diet and keep it as clean as possible—and what my kids would class as a cheat sheet or life hack—is the following.

Choose only foods that have either:

- $ **grown from the ground.**
- $ **fallen from a tree.**
- $ **walked the earth.**

Avoid adding sugar, salt, sauces, and processed foods, and your mind will soon reflect and be your best friend in achieving your goals, dreams, and ambitions. It is also a very good idea to avoid alcohol for a week prior to the pitch, and just to be a super Grinch, I would also add coffee to that list. If not for the whole week, for sure avoid it on the day. You do not want to be walking into that room with the caffeine jitters!

Having a healthy, balanced, correctly nour-ished body will shine through in the boardroom and give you the best possible chance at the perfect presentation.

Please note before embarking on any new food plan or diet that it's important to speak with your doctor or health care provider. As much as this is a disclaimer, I also advise this in general. Getting a full blood count to check where your levels are currently sitting will show you what your starting point is. Revisit the doctor on his or her advice, but I would definitely advise a checkup after six weeks. If you adopt this new healthy way of living it is great to see the results for yourself and be able to give yourself a pat on the back!

5.3 MUSIC

The power of music is amazing. It is boundless, and there is always something new to discover. It is an incredibly powerful tool for evoking emotions and influencing people, but did you know it can also be used to instantly flip the switch on your brainwaves, moving you from beta to alpha within a few beats of the tune? This is why some of the best speakers and performers in the world use music prior to a performance to place their mindset into optimum condition to present. Some have a genre, but most have a certain playlist or a few songs that are guaranteed to push them right where they need to be.

This is due to a number of factors. Firstly, it helps you focus. Listening to something that gives you pleasure will help remove any negative distractions. It's hard to think of the bad things in your life while blasting out lyrics like,

"DON'T WORRY, BE HAPPY!"

While you are enjoying the pleasures of your tunes, your body is busy releasing the neurotransmitter dopamine, your natural feel-good drug.

The selection of the soundtrack is important. You want to be entering the alpha state and not the gamma state. Think about the music you listen to and how it makes you feel. You want it to be making you feel more powerful, grounded, calm, and strong as opposed to feeling pumped, wild, and explosive.

Just think about it like going to the gym. There are certain songs, albums, or playlists that are guaranteed to give you that extra boost on the treadmill or extra couple of reps of the barbell. These tunes are different for everyone. My husband and I both have a motivational playlist; however, the songs, artists, and genres are polar opposite. Therefore, when selecting your pre-pitch song selection, choose for you and how it makes you feel. Play the list on the way to the pitch, and save your ultimate number-one song for just before you enter the room. Then keep that beat in your head.

I WALK IN THE ROOM TO MY TUNE!

5.4 EXERCISE

Mentioning gyms brings me nicely onto arguably one of the most beneficial things you can do, not only for your performance, but also for your overall mental and physical health in general. Even in as little as ten minutes a day, a person can start to feel improvements in their mental state and their physical health.

There are many books written by people, including myself, on the benefits of exercise for physical health. But do you know the benefits of physical fitness for your mental health and brain strength? Just twenty minutes of your heart pumping everyday can improve your brain's information-processing functions exponentially. It also expels stress hormones and provides you with an abundance of happy hormones, giving you that natural high.

To be clear, I am not suggesting that you run twenty minutes around the block before entering the room to present your pitch. That would only create a sweaty mess and an uncomfortable situation for you and the potential investor—and no doubt an unpleasant odor in the room! However, on the buildup to the big day try to get at least twenty minutes, but ideally one hour, of a mix of cardio and strength training in four to five times per week. The mix of getting your heart rate up and strengthening your muscles will not only ensure your mental health improves, but along with the feel-good factor of exercise you'll also feel better about yourself.

When you take care of your physical body, you can start to see changes. The longer you practice good physical well-being the more improvements you will visibly be able to see. When you look in the mirror and you like what you see, you'll feel proud of yourself for the work you have put in, and your confidence will grow.

The effects of growing confidence will start a waterfall effect. When you are proud of your body you'll look after it more. You may find yourself dressing better and taking more pride in your appearance. Now while this is only a small part of the overall package it is definitely an area that will bode well for you when it comes to first impressions in the boardroom.

SO ON THE RUN UP TO THE BIG DAY GET OUT, GET MOVING, AND HEY, KEEP IT UP AFTERWARD. YOU WILL THANK YOURSELF FOR IT!

5.5 SLEEP

The importance and correct amount of sleep have been much-discussed and debated topics over the years, yet the importance of a good night's sleep is still an aspect of our lives that is still hugely overlooked.

When it comes to achieving optimum physical and mental states, the right amount and quality of sleep is absolutely essential. When it comes to achieving an optimal state for planning and presentation, a full, proper night's sleep will play an important role in ensuring your mood, memory, data retention, and judgment are at their peak. The human body was designed to be recharged daily. During sleep we are able to fully rest, heal, and restructure. If your body doesn't rest and heal you are more likely to develop mood problems, health problems, and even serious illness such as diabetes and stroke down the line.

A good night's sleep is not just about going to bed and closing your eyes. It begins with a good evening and nighttime routine that should begin about two to three hours before bedtime. This is as true for adults as it is for children. This is especially true in the current age of technology.

Humans are designed to recognize when it is nighttime, and when it is the body begins to prepare itself to recharge. The darkness, the moon, and the quiet all tell the body that it will soon be resting time. However, modern stimulants like phones, iPads, laptops, TVs, as well as food and alcohol all contribute to the disruption of this natural process.

If you are spending the two hours prior to bed-time drinking wine, eating pizza, and watching movies while playing with your phone, you are confusing your natural instincts into thinking it should still be awake, and it remains in a stimulation phase—a beta wave.

In order for it to accept that it will be entering the delta wave, you have to prepare the brain in advance. Don't eat within two hours of bedtime. Swap the glass of wine for a nice, calming tea. Put the phone away, turn off the TV, and grab yourself a book. Reading a book will transition you into the alpha state, making delta much easier to achieve. The results of this will be a good, proper night's sleep and a brain ready to take on the world the next morning.

As with all the steps, the results are not individual to each action. Good sleep will assist you achieving all the other aspects of perfect mindset. A lack of sleep is proven to reduce your willpower and will make you more likely to turn to your comfort zone, resulting in poor choices in nutrition and well-being. A lack of sleep will make you more likely to skip the workout, choose the easier options, and opt for the fast foods over what you know are the healthy choices.

Achieving prolonged healthy sleep patterns will keep you alert, reduce your stress, and improve your memory. Basically, sleep is your money can't buy brain medicine, and it's available to everyone! So switch off your television, turn your phone on silent, pour a nice cup of tea, dim the lights, and settle into a good book. Come pitch day you will be diamond!

5.6 SUN

Let me be more specific here. I am talking vitamin D and getting outside into the fresh air. Over the past few years (the Covid years), people were put under incredibly strict rules, many of which were incredibly detrimental to the health of our minds, bodies, and souls. Some of these rules involved limiting or even banning outdoor activity completely. This restriction of fresh air and lack of exposure to vitamin D via sunlight was terrible for our mental and physical health. The sun is a powerful weapon for strengthening our bodies and our immune systems, as well as being an incredible booster for our mental health.

The benefits of sun exposure are often overlooked as the discussions based around sun are usually about keeping out if it, using sunscreen, and the constant fear of skin cancer. What isn't discussed as often is how incredibly good sun is for us.

ONE OF THE BEST AND EASIEST WAYS TO INCREASE YOUR VITAMIN D IS TO GET OUTSIDE.

Vitamin D promotes strong bones and supports your muscles, nerves, and immune system. When your body is exposed to the sun it is easier for it to transition from daytime to nighttime. When you have had significant sun exposure and then recognize the sunsets, your body produces its own supply of melatonin. Melatonin is critical for a good night's sleep, so the better your sun routine, the better your sleep will be. Melatonin also reduces stress. Keeping your supply regular and natural will keep your stress hormones at bay. Along with melatonin, sunlight exposure increases your serotonin.

An increased natural supply of serotonin will immediately benefit your brain function, sleep, memory, and sexual behavior; ward off depression; subside emotional hunger pains; and in general just make you a happier person. And it should go without say that happier people are much better at selling themselves in the boardroom!

5.7 SCREEN TIME

There are over 5.3 billion people in the world today who own cell phones. The average American daily use time is almost four hours per day. With the majority of the time being spent scrolling social media sites, humanity is becoming addicted to instant news stories and watching others. Social media has been associated with a rapid increase in physical, emotional, and mental issues. It can have severe detrimental effects on our interpersonal social abilities, self-esteem, and sleep quality. Limiting your social media and monitoring how much time you are spending scrolling will bring back your awareness and allow you to focus on what is important.

When it comes to your pitch, try to avoid scrolling on your phone the day of the presentation. Not only will this allow the benefits of all the other work you have put in to shine through, but it will also eliminate the risk of unwanted distraction or clickbait that will deviate your focus away from the task at hand. This is your time, and you don't want to be thinking about skateboarding babies, fighting students, or people doing mean things to cats as you prepare for this important moment.

Better still, turning off your phone completely for at least three hours before you enter the room will get that mind focused and prepared in the best possible way and will ensure that you are giving your best pitch ever!

SUMMARY
MINDSET

§ Confidence is key, and the key to confidence is knowledge.

§ Meditation— Practice shifting your state of mind between brainwaves.

§ Eat well— The healthier the body, the healthier the mind.

§ Music— Use your favorite tunes to optimize your state of mind.

§ Exercise— Get into the habit of daily exercise to improve your mind, body, and soul.

§ Sleep— Prepare your mind every night to ensure the perfect night's sleep.

§ Sun— Sun is your friend, enjoy exposure daily for maximum health benefits

§ Screen time— Limit your screen time in order to limit your chances of mind manipulation.

CHAPTER SIX

ACCOUNTABILITY

WHAT DOES IT MEAN TO BE ACCOUNTABLE?

Try standing in a room full of people and ask them,

"WHO IN THIS ROOM IS ACCOUNTABLE?"

You will immediately feel the energy in the room switch. The temperature will rise, and you will soon feel like you are facing the line-up in *The Usual Suspects*. Everyone will start looking at one another with an "It wasn't me; was it you?" kind of stare. All you have mentioned is the adjective, no mention of any noun, but everyone has instantly associated the sentence with a negative. It immediately fills people with doubt and fear. Accountability is basically accepting responsibility for your own actions so if I ask, *Who is accountable?*

I AM MERELY ASKING WHO IS RESPONSIBLE FOR THEIR OWN ACTIONS.

One of the greatest qualities of a leader is accountability, and one of the top qualities of the world's best fundraising consultants is their leadership skills. This is because we often hold the same values. As CEO of a successful security company and a fundraising consultant, I rely on the same qualities when it comes to running a business as I do when asking for money: integrity, communication, self-awareness, gratitude, influence, courage, respect, empathy, and above all, accountability.

One of my life mantras has and will always be,

THE BUCK STOPS HERE.

In fact my own family, whether it be my six-year-old or my husband, knows that we make our own beds, we clean our own rooms, and we fight our own battles. We are accountable for all our own actions.

Planning a successful donation or investment pitch comes with that same level of accountability. Whether you are doing it on your own or working with a team of people, you have to ensure the responsibilities are clear and each person knows what they are accountable for. If you are the person stepping into the room to do the pitch, then the buck definitely lies with you. You are the representative of this pitch, and you will be the symbol of the charity or business in the face of the donor.

WHAT DOES THIS REALLY MEAN?

It means that you are responsible for all your own actions, but you are also accountable for what the team around you does. You have to ensure each person has been tasked with completing the job that best suits his or her abilities. If team members are out of their depths, struggling, and not accepting their own responsibilities you will end up in a bad situation.

What if you don't realize a mistake from your team until you are standing in a boardroom in front of the judge and jury of your pitch, reading those notes they have prepared for you. What will inevitably happen is the doubts, fears, anxieties, and nerves will hit you like a ton of bricks. Those old fears of failing will be in full flow.

Therefore, the responsibility and accountably of this lies firmly at your door. Sure, you can go back and chastise the intern who had no idea what they were actually meant to be doing, but it really makes no difference. The opportunity you worked so hard for has gone, and second chances in the world of money are not plentiful.

Let's look at an example. I was running a very high-profile fundraising campaign. During a planning meeting I was reviewing each person's individual tasks. It was four months until the challenge was due to start, and the director was concerned I was going to risk microman-agement. I had informed him my gut feeling was telling me that all was not going as well as what was being portrayed and that I needed to be sure each task had been completed.

Now, this wasn't my responsibility, but the success of the task, the reputation of the campaign, and the money raised for the charity was all my responsibility, so by proxy, every-one else's tasks were also my responsibility.

One individual had been assigned two tasks. He informed me that all was in hand and not to worry. I wasn't satisfied, so I probed. He took severe offense to my probing and threw everything at me, including his position in his business, the respect from his peers, the facts he was male and older, his life experience, the fact he had bigger feet than me. (OK, that's an exaggeration, but you get my drift.)

I remained calm and explained that all his qualities were very impressive and that's why we are delighted to be working with him, but that it would be remiss of me to not check. If I didn't I would feel I wasn't doing my job properly. He squirmed a little more and really tried to deflect.

It would have been incredibly easy for me to just accept his word and sit down feeling intimidated, but you have to fully understand your own values. If accountability is one, then feeling uncomfortable is not an excuse. Once he realized I wasn't budging, and without actually saying that he hadn't completed the tasks, he quickly switched his defense from being that he was fully capable and shouldn't be questioned, to it being everyone else's fault that he had been under so much pressure. It was impossible for him to have ever completed the tasks assigned to him. He blamed me, his director, and the other people on the team and refused to bear any responsibility for himself.

If I had not trusted my gut and held true to my own accountability for the overall success of the campaign, he would have carried on the way he was going, and inevitability failed. His failure would have rippled down within the group, and failure for one would have been failure for everyone.

When it comes to your own fundraising campaign, **accountability is key.** Once the opportunity is gone, it's gone, so as much as there is no time for regrets there is no time for:

$ **That's not my job.**

$ **That's his responsibility.**

$ **She should have done that.**

If this is your pitch, then you are accountable for all your own actions, but also be sure that you have delegated correctly and that every piece of the puzzle is actioned properly.

Remember:

THE BUCK STOPS WITH YOU!

SUMMARY
ACCOUNTABILITY

$ Accountability is accepting responsibility for one's own actions.

$ Failure for one is failure for everyone.

$ No room for excuses, egos or regrets when it comes to a successful result.

$ The buck stops with you.

CHAPTER SEVEN

PLANNING

Planning and preparation are the most important steps in any operation, whether that be business, running a campaign, conducting a military operation, or even your everyday events. If you don't get the planning stage correct, you'll forever be on the back foot. My husband is a military man, and he was the one who introduced me to the seven Ps.

PRIOR PLANNING AND PREPARATION PREVENT PISS-POOR PERFORMANCE.

The planning stage is key to giving yourself every chance at the best possible result; however, just like entering the battlefield, the best plans only survive first contact, so you should be prepared for every eventuality. This means knowing your five Ws for every aspect of your mission.

WHAT, WHY, WHO, WHERE, AND WHEN.

The more knowledge you have going into your pitch, the more effective it will be. So what should you know, and what do the five Ws mean?

There are five key elements you should KNOW to ensure perfect planning, and to have full knowledge you should understand the five Ws of each KNOW. These elements are:

1. **Your Ask**
2. **Your Audience**
3. **Your Product**
4. **Your Team**
5. **Your Win**

Let's look into each of these elements in more detail.

1. **KNOW your ask.** What are you asking for? Why are you asking for it? Who will it benefit? Where will it be distributed? When do you need it?

This seems like an incredibly obvious piece of knowledge to have, but you would be surprised how many people have no idea what they are asking for. They walk into the boardroom, stand in front of their potential donors, and ask for support. The first question is asked. "What are you asking for?"

And all they can respond with is something like, "Well … I'm asking for your help?"

The pitcher has no idea what they are really even asking for. They don't know exactly what they need, how much of it they need, what the timelines are, or anything else for that matter.

Knowing in full what you're asking for specifically will help you and the donor establish exactly the kind of relationship you want from the get-go. The relationship should be clear, defined, and specific, not wishy-washy.

Know exactly what you are asking for. If it is solely for one payment, know the exact amount, why you want it, where you will use it, and when you need it. If it is regular donations, again know how much, where it will be distributed, and when each payment is needed.

Write all this down, and be really specific with yourself. Make sure it is accurate. It may even be worth enlisting the help of a financial expert to ensure you are correct in your assumptions of what you need. The more you understand what you're asking for, the easier it will be fcr the person sitting in front of you to understand. You should be able to answer any question they may pose. Some investors and donors are laid-back and just want to hear about getting the best return on investment or how much of a tax write-off they can do.

Others, and I would say the majority, want details. They want the details for their own knowledge, shareholders' knowledge, and most importantly, people who deal with money want to know the people they are getting into bed with are smart, savvy, and will produce a return.

A person who stumbles through a pitch with "I'll have to check that out," "Let me get back to you on that," or "I'm not quite sure, I don't know," is not someone they want to be doing business with. If you don't know these answers by the time you have walked into their room, when do you ever plan on learning? Therefore,

KNOW YOUR ASK!

2. **KNOW your audience.** Who are they? What do they do? Why are these the people you're talking to? Where are their passions compared to your ask? When is the best time to pitch to them?

The aim here is to know them better than they know themselves. You want to know who they are, what their company policies are, whether they have a CSR (corporate social responsibility) plan and if so, whether your ask aligns with their principals. If it doesn't, can you adapt? Are you talking to the right people?

You don't want to waste your time talking to the wrong person, as much as they don't want their time wasted. There is zero point in pitching an anti-gun fundraising campaign to the NRA or a Greenpeace initiative to oil tycoons, just as there is little point to wasting your well-rehearsed pitch on a middleman with no sway.

You want to be in the room with the decision makers every time. Even if the middleman says he will pass everything on, no one else can pitch this like your well-rehearsed self. Always be polite, but let it be known you are willing to wait for the CEO, the COO, or the person with the decision-making abilities.

As a final note on knowing your audience, always know when a good time is to be asking. When is the end of their financial year? When do they allocate funding? When are they going live on the stock market? When is their next big product launch? Your timings of the ask are just as crucial as knowing who you are asking.

Remember during an interview, when the question of what you know about the company arises, it is asked to see how much you care and how much time you have put into it—how much you really want the job. This is no different. How much do you want this investment? When you are confident in your pitch and are able to display full knowledge of the company you are pitching to, they will immediately feel more relaxed when they feel you understand and know them.

KNOW YOUR AUDIENCE.

3. **KNOW your product.** What are you offering? Who are you/the brand? Why do
   you stand out from the rest? Where is your
   brand today? When were you discovered,
   and what is your story?

This is another obvious one but again one that
is overlooked. It doesn't matter if you are
selling a product, asking for an investment,
or seeking a donation, it is imperative when
you stand in front of the investor that you
know your product inside out.

What is it you are offering?

If this is a physical object, it is a lot easier to describe. Think of shows like *Shark
Tank* and *Dragon's Den*. Could you imagine if
they stood up in front of the panel, having
no idea what their product was or what it did?
There is no difference when you are asking for
money. They will want to know what they are
buying. What are they investing in? What makes
your offering different from all the other nonprofits in your field? Why should they pick you
over them?

Know your story, your background, what has
brought you here today. I have spoken to many

fundraisers who tell me, for example, they're raising money to eliminate childhood cancer.

Great! A fantastic cause. "Tell me about your charity," I say.

There's a long pause before they reply, "Well, we are trying to end childhood cancer."

This is not enough. I need to know why you are doing it, what your motivation is, and what your story is. History tells an investor a lot about the future and will determine whether they are willing to take a bet on you.

Knowing your brand, your product, and what you are selling—not just on the surface, but every level of that product from conception to now—will satisfy the investor that you are serious and worth taking a punt on. Every piece of knowledge you have is another weapon in your arsenal.

KNOW YOUR PRODUCT!

4. **KNOW your team.** What motivates them? Who are they? Why have they been chosen for their positions? When did they get involved, and when will they leave? Where are they going?

Who are you working with? This is as important to know in the boardroom as it is in the everyday operations of your business or cause. Understanding individual motivations and drives will help you decide where they are best served.

You have to know if they are in it for the long haul or if this is just a passing job for them, something to fill a gap. Not everyone will have the drive and commitment that you have, especially if this is your brand or your cause.

If you are the person who set this up or are driven by this cause, it will pump through your veins night and day. This will most likely not be true for every other member of your team. Of course you are able to inspire and motivate them to have passion and drive to champion the cause, but no one can love your baby like you do.

It is important to remember this when selecting who will go into the room for the pitch to sell your offering. Most would automatically discard the person who is there solely for the paycheck, the one who isn't the leader, isn't the driver, who does a good job but switches off as soon as he leaves the office. However, this can sometimes be a mistake or an overlook, depending on who he or she is. They may actually be the best person you have for the pitch. These types of employees are usually objective, unbiased and logical in their thinking.

They are not emotionally invested like you are, not financially incentivized like some of your other employees, and would be able to deliver a factual presentation lacking in nerves and adrenaline.

That employee may be just as good as the over-enthusiastic, supermotivated employee-of-the-month, especially if he or she follows the formula and has all the information required to answer anything that is throw at them. They can deal with this in a purely logical and completely professional and levelheaded way.

The important thing is knowing your team, their motivations, their strengths, and their weaknesses. The whole team around you must be in their optimal position, whether that is research, planning, administration, or the actual person who will walk into the room, placing them correctly is key. Making sure they all follow the basics in this book both as individuals and as a team gives you the strongest possible chance at the win.

KNOW YOUR TEAM!

5. **KNOW your win.** What does success look like? Who are the winners? Why was it a success? When do you win? Where do you go from there?

Visualization of what you really want is everything, yet so many just go through the process hoping for the best, satisfied by any outcome. While those searching for business investments are usually better at this than nonprofit fundraisers, it is still an area that is neglected.

You may believe in the law of attraction, the power of prayer, angels, manifestations, or sacrifice. Whatever it is you believe, in order for the higher power to deliver, they first need to know what you want. "The best you can give" doesn't cut it with the greats. They want specifics! What does it look like when you achieve your goals?

There is a famous—or infamous some might say—study conducted by a prestigious US school about goal setting. Prior to graduation, a class was asked about their goals, and 84 percent of the class had set goals but not written down. Just 13 percent had set written goals but had no plan for how to achieve them, while the remaining 3 percent had written down their goals and had a clear plan.

Now many people over the years have disputed this study as myth; however, from my experience, even if the study itself is a myth, the outcome is as true as if it were factual. The 13 percent of the class who had written down their goals achieved them at double the rate of the 84 percent who had not wrote them down. The 3 percent who had written down their goals and had a plan to achieve them were achieving at ten times the rate of the 97 percent.

This may well be urban myth, but what's to say you can't try it yourself. Set yourself a small goal, write it down, and make a plan to achieve it. I guarantee you are ten times more likely to achieve it than by having no plan at all!

Therefore, when you enter that room, know what winning looks like. What will the funds achieve, who is benefitting from them, and how will their lives look when they have this benefit? Tell the investor the story of what difference building the school will make or how finding that cure for the illness will change lives. What will your new business look like when it is up and running, and how will it change the community?

Share your vision with them, and help them see it. They really want to know this if you have managed to touch their hearts. If you can tap into their imagination and really paint that picture, you will be many steps closer to achieving your outcome.

KNOW YOUR WIN.

SUMMARY

$ The planning stage is all about knowledge. You cannot have enough of it.

$ Study, adapt, and embed your plan, and make it part of your day-to-day work.

$ Make sure your team is also equipped with this knowledge. It may come second nature to you, but that might not be the case for everyone.

$ Study, practice, rehearse, test, and repeat until it becomes second nature to everyone.

$ You can never be overprepared when it comes to planning. This is definitely an area where more is more.

CHAPTER EIGHT
STRATEGY

Once you have the planning nailed down, it is important to have a strategy. Walking into the room and presenting with an explosion of verbal diarrhea will put potential donors off as quickly as walking into the room and saying nothing would.

You have to know how you are going to present and know it as well as a theater director presenting a play on Broadway. It has to go effortlessly, smoothly and make the viewer fall in love. The strategy incorporates your planning with your performance and your presentation. Put this all together and you will have even the toughest critic begging for an encore!

Understanding the following six steps will help you when it comes to planning your strategy.

8.1 SALES

Be under no illusions; asking for money is a sales pitch. Hundreds if not thousands of books have been written on the topic of how to sell. Each decade seems to bring on a new technique or trick of the trade, promising earnings of tens of thousands of dollars in your first thirty days of training. Let's face it: most of them were bullshit. But to be fair to history, there were some interesting methods out there.

If you ever worked in sales, especially in the nineties, you will be very familiar with the age-old technique of interviewers asking new candidates to "sell me this pen." This technique has been used for decades to demonstrate how great a salesperson someone is. Following the release of the movie *The Wolf of Wall Street* it became popular as a tool for identifying the ultimate salesperson.

Now, while I agree this is a good (not great) tool for demonstrating things like confidence, fast-thinking, and how well a person can bullshit on their feet, it is not a method I would ever use when teaching long-term successful sales skills. I would also hazard a guess that The Wolf himself would secretly agree with me.

You see, someone babbling on about how amazing this pen is, a pen they know nothing about, having just held it for the first time, usually doesn't tell me anything about them other than how much crap they are able to talk about a tube of ink.

Jordan Belfort himself famously teaches the three tens in sales. If you are unfamiliar with this, the three tens are the confidence level out of ten of three key factors, including:

- $ **the product being sold,**
- $ **the person they are talking to,**
- $ **the company behind the product.**

By his own definition, the **sell-me-a-pen** technique is the opposite of these golden rules.

Being a successful salesperson requires the perfect mix of confidence, accountability, knowledge, and strategy. Sure, thinking on your feet is useful, but knowledge will outsell bullshit every time. Being good at sales is about knowing your product, knowing your company, and knowing your customer.

The more you know, the better you will be at selling. It should now be clear that the skills required to be the perfect salesperson are the same skills that are required to be successful when it comes to asking for money.

At thirteen I gained my first taste of the sales environment. My older brother had been looking for a job and found one in the news-paper for a telemarketer position. The salary wasn't great— in fact it was next to nothing; however, the possible commission was more money than he or I had ever seen. The issue came when he was too nervous to pick up the phone and make the call— not a great start for a career in telemarketing.

So I picked up the phone, called them up, and asked about the position. I explained I was calling on behalf of my brother who was look-ing for work. It wasn't long into the conversa-tion before the lady in charge was offering me the job. Apparently she admired my confidence and telephone manner. I explained I was only thirteen, and she explained she could pay in cash. That was music to my ears. I was in, and I got my brother in too.

The job of a telesales operator was very simple I read from a script, got the customer to agree they were interested in purchasing windows/doors/timeshares whatever it was, and then I passed the lead on to the salesman. I was paid for every lead I passed over and extra if the sale progressed (something that was very rare). There were about thirty people working in the office over three-hour shifts, and I constantly watched and learned from everyone there.

The first thing that struck me at thirteen was how some people could end the three hours with twenty to thirty leads, while others were lucky to get one. More often than not, the poor performers blamed everything they possibly could as an excuse for their poor returns.

The things I heard people blame over the years included: their phone lists were poor, the customers were not right, everyone they spoke to had just bought windows yesterday, their phone wasn't the right color, and more.

I MEAN IF THERE WAS AN EXCUSE AVAILABLE, THEY WOULD USE IT.

The one thing I never saw them do, however, was approach the high performers and ask them for advice, ask how they were doing it, ask what their secrets were.

The reason for this was explained in chapter 4, "Fear." They did not want to admit any failures, be embarrassed, or feel out of control. There was a handful of very successful people in the group, and each one of them had learned from the others. They began with the basics: no closed questions, smile while you talk, and believe in the sale. Then they moved on to the more advanced individual skills.

The truth is every person in the room had the ability to take away twenty to thirty leads a day; however, with the refusals to utilize the resources in front of them, they instead chose to confirm the old saying that a poor workman always blames his tools.

The top salesperson in the office was the one I made the beeline for. She was Australian and had long, surfer-blonde hair, a nose ring, clothes made from hemp, an infectious smile, and confidence that made everyone gravitate toward her.

She would be sitting at her desk shouting at her boyfriend (who also worked in the office), smoking cigarette after cigarette as the most vulgar language poured from her mouth as she dialed her calls.

THEN THE CLIENT WOULD ANSWER.

The change was instant. This beaming smile stretched across her face, and she was in the zone. That smile seemed to be her on-switch. Every other salesperson had a script in front of them, but not her.

She told me as her first piece of advice: "Take this home and learn it. Learn it until you are repeating it in your head walking down the street. Everyone on the other end of the phone can spot a script—it's like talking to a robot. We don't buy things we don't want from robots."

That brings me to my next biggest excuse I hear from poor salesmen. "But no one I spoke to today wanted windows and doors. I can't force them".

That's a huge rookie mistake. Everyone on that phone had windows and doors in their house, and everyone wants an upgrade. I don't care who you are: if something can be improved in your house, you can be convinced by the right person to improve it. This is true in life and business too.

You see, the key difference between the bubbly Australian surfer chick and the egotistical curtain-haired yuppy who couldn't sell, wasn't that she was better than him from the start or that she was hotter or smoother than him, and it wasn't that she was given easier leads.

NONE OF THAT MATTERS IN SALES.

What did matter was when she was given the job, she took those scripts home, studied them, and learned until she was saying them in her sleep. She took home the window-and-door manuals and studied them. She searched through previous leads, learned trends in local areas, and utilized human nature, like keeping up with the Joneses. She didn't just see her job as existing just during those three hours. She saw that there was money to be made, and if she put the hours in outside of the three on the sales floor, then she would be rewarded tenfold. She had a strategy, and she developed it.

8.2 IT'S A BUSINESS

Sales, simply put, is a business transaction between two people. Investing and fundraising are no different. It is all business and should be treated as such.

Someone asked me during the process of writing this book whether it was aimed at charities or businesses, and I replied simply that it was a book about how to ask for money.

They repeated their question, asking if it was aimed at nonprofits or for-profits. Right there I thanked them, as they had just given me a whole subchapter of the book. Their mere persistence at repeating the question told me there is a general lack of understanding about the art of fundraising. If I haven't said it loudly enough, let me repeat myself.

FUNDRAISING IS A BUSINESS!

A familiar statement to fundraising consultants is, "How can you charge for helping a charity?" Well, for fundraising consultants, this is their business—a craft they have perfected—and they are usually very good at it.

Would you ask your accountant, your banker, or your kids' teachers to work for free?

In fact, statement like, "How can you charge for helping a charity?" are the very words that will show people like me you are not approaching the process the correct way. You are seeing this as a cause and working from the heart. You are not seeing this as a campaign that requires strategy, management, and planning. Furthermore, and most importantly, you are about to make the biggest mistake in fundraising—**focusing everything on the sob story**.

This situation is insanely common in fundraising campaigns all across the world—the focus is purely on the cause. *Well of course*, I hear you say, *the cause is the most important part of fundraising*. Wrong. The cause is the most important part of fundraising to *you*, but to donors, this is a business transaction.

They are giving this money to you, and most people expect something in return when they hand over their hard-earned cash. You are starting a sales process, and as we have already established, people do transactions with people, not causes.

They want you to convince them why this is a good idea and how it will benefit **them.** How does this transaction enhance their lives? This benefit may be formed in many different ways, but without a doubt, whether you are pitching to a corporation or a private individual, they will want to know they have skin in the game.

Empathy isn't enough. They need to be solving a specific problem. That problem may be to settle inner guilt, to tick a box on the company social responsibility data, to satisfy a personal need, or to complete a job spec. Whatever the reason the donor wants to know what's in it for them. This is business. (Have I said that already?) No matter how much you believe in your cause, to the person across the desk, this is almost always business.

I will note here that there is a slight exception for this, and that is at live events, auctions, and gala fundraisers. Here you are very much focused on the art of persuasion in impulse buying. This is where some of the sell-me-the-pen skills will come more into play. I will talk more about this in chapter 15.

By now you should have no doubt that what you are doing needs to be dealt with the head and not the heart. The next stage is to know what they want to know and how to provide the answers.

8.3 BE SPECIFIC

Once you have answered all the investors' questions regarding the ask and satisfied their needs and returns, your next stage is to satisfy their need for knowledge. They want to know where the money is going, and this is where they'll want specifics. The best advice here is to be as on point as you can be, no more and no less. People want to really know where their money is going, and everyone loves their dose of glory.

During one of my campaigns, fundraising for a mental health collaboration, we knew that every dollar we raised meant one more telephone call would be answered in the children's mental health helpline. We were able to use that specific statistic in our conversations with donors. But again, we used facts and figures. We discussed the helpline, the need for it, and how funds would be used to benefit the children. If you are looking for someone to invest in something, there will always be a requirement for specific details.

Whether you are asking someone to invest in an opportunity, a large-scale project, a new business, or to donate money to a cause, the donor will always want to know at least the very basic specifics. In fundraising it will be formed on developing the cause, what the funds will do for the charity, what recognition the donor will receive, and the amount needed for each achievement.

Similarly to when you'd ask someone to invest in a new business, they will want to know the business plans, the financials, the competition, the standout details, and the marketing strategies.

If you have ever watched one of those shows where new startups pitch to a panel of investors or compete with other businesspeople for a job, you may be familiar with some of the people they turn away, who don't receive the investments and don't get the job. It is always the ones who are not specific. The don't know their stats, their resumes are all over the place, their cashflow plans or valuations are completely off the scale, or simply put, they just don't know!

Not only does this lack of specifics display a lack of knowledge in your pitch, but it also advertises laziness. Wanting to know the specifics of where they are investing their cash is not only very normal, but it's also a major requirement of most investors. If you don't have that information at hand, do you expect them to go and find these answers? Would you like them to spend their time as well as their money doing your job?

Make it easy for them. Asking for money may give you nerves, but fear of delivery should not. The more knowledge you have, the more power you have. My number-one tip here is: **Always know as much as possible about the subject, and be able to answer more questions in your pitch than they could ever ask.**

8.4 CONFIDENCE

Remember the Australian girl from my tele-marketing days? What made her so successful wasn't her beautiful smile and awesome personality. No, her biggest asset was her overt confidence. It's possible this came from her beauty and carefree character, but I would argue that her vast knowledge, her time spent studying, and her lack of nerves about questions was what gave her the confidence.

Confidence shines through as much as nerves and apprehension do, but if you don't have a natural confidence, how do you create it?

Confidence is all about security, no matter the task at hand. If you are secure in the subject, your ability to present or perform will be greatly increased as you have the confidence. You have worked through the fears, set forth your plans, and are in the right mindset to win.

Having a firm strategy, a strong knowledge of your client, sound comprehension of what you're selling, and really knowing what you are talking about will inevitably give you a strong confidence in your ability to make the person in front of you want what you have. In turn you will get that investment you are asking for.

Using all the tools I created in the MAPS formula won't necessarily give you that confidence to be first in line for karaoke at the next office party, but it will give you confidence in what you need to deliver, which will eliminate the nerves that come with being unprepared.

8.5 THE POWER OF SILENCE

Having confidence will also stop you from rambling. There is nothing worse than getting to the end of the pitch, and the pitcher keeps going, keeps filling the small silences. Slowly but surely, he then begins to talk himself out of the sale.

THE POWER OF SILENCE SHOULD NEVER BE UNDERESTIMATED.

The silent pause is one of the most powerful tools you can enlist in your arsenal. I have often watched a presentation go on and on, never ending the conversation, even after making the pitch in full. The speaker is simply unable to close. In fact, silence in general terrifies people. Most people can barely last a few seconds in the presence of silence.

However, the power of that pause, that quiet battle of who will make the first move, who will draw first, gives the winner an incredible upper hand. In some cultures, the silent power is considered incredibly powerful and can teach your opponent a lot about what you're made of.

The art of listening is heavily overlooked. Many think that during a pitch they have to deliver as much information as they possibly can. They forget natural human abilities like attention spans, the need to question, and the necessity to be respected.

Silence allows for deeper reflection and thoughtfulness. Constant chatter does not give your potential client time to think or digest what you have said. This is particularly important after you have delivered crucial or brand-new information. Give them time to digest.

Practice with your colleagues or friends. Start with one or two seconds, and work your way up to eight to ten. Identify the point at which you became uncomfortable, and practice removing that discomfort. The more you introduce the silent pause, the easier it will become. Believe me when I say you will soon be enjoying your newfound silent superpower.

8.6 APPROACH

Once you have built up the strategy for your pitch, it is time to deliver it. This stage needs just as much of a strategy. Think of an aspiring singer running around New York with their mixed tape trying to hand it off to music execs, ambushing them as they leave the office, or the incredibly annoying salesperson in the store who approaches you as soon as you step through the door, you know the one.

"HI, HOW ARE YOU? HOW CAN I HELP YOU? ARE YOU LOOKING FOR ANYTHING IN PARTICULAR TODAY?"

Even when you tell them you are happy just to browse, they still watch you all the way around the store, ready to pounce at the slightest hint of eye contact. You are barely able to focus on the shopping as you're too busy planning your quick getaway the minute they drop their guard.

You have focused so much on avoiding them that you forgot what you came for in the first place, and all you care about is getting out unscathed. Their approach completely ruins your shopping experience, and going forward you actively avoid that store. It goes back to that very important first impression, and if you blow that, you rarely get a second chance.

First impressions are all about building a relationship. This stage is not a transaction, but where you make them feel at ease and comfortable in your presence. There is a huge difference between relationship-building and business transactions, and it is important that you keep each stage separate. Introduce the latter at the right time to ensure the crossover is smooth and doesn't crosscontaminate.

This is where you pull everything you learned in MAPS together —mindset, accountability, planning, and strategy. This will ensure that your approach happens at the right time, in the right tone, with all the information required, and with a confident mindset.

You have all the tools to open your pitch and close just at the right times. Your introductions may be cold or via a recommendation, they may approach you or you may approach them; however, having **MAPS** in your back pocket will bring you closer to success than you have ever been.

PART 3

GIVEN—AFTER THE GIVE

CHAPTER NINE
INTRODUCTION TO GIVEN

Months of planning and hard work are done. You have erased all of the fears, followed the MAPS formula, nailed the meeting, and the money is in the bank!

The hard work is over, and your job is done …

RIGHT?

Unfortunately, even for the best of the best in the industry, this is still one of the biggest faux pas made by fundraisers.

Imagine this scenario: You are a CFO of a multimillion-dollar empire. (You choose what business you envision.) You have reached this level of the game because it is a business you are incredibly passionate about. You have worked hard to get there, spending days and nights building this business, you have sac-rificed time with your family, faced the highs and the lows, and put your all in to get it where it is.

In fact, it's so successful you now have people coming to you asking you to invest in their businesses or make substantial donations to their causes. It's a good feeling, right?

Then you take time out of your very busy day to listen to many pitches, and one in particular really stands out. You decide that is the one you are going to invest in. You write out the check and hand it over to a very excited recipient. You feel good. You have just made a difference, and it's a good feeling.

But soon that initial adrenaline starts to dissipate, and you are now left wondering what has happened with your investment. What differences has it made? Who have you helped? You have heard nothing for weeks, and your initial buzz has turned to bewilderment and even resentment.

They really wanted your help and put a lot of effort into securing it, and now that you have helped them you have been dropped, no expressions of thanks, nc updates on the investment, no contact whatsoever—not even a bunch of flowers.

IT SUCKS!

There is a mix of feelings happening now. You may feel pretty pissed off and used. You may feel rejected, no longer needed, or insignificant. You may even forget why you helped them in the first place. One thing is for sure though, especially if this is your first time as a donor, you have learned a big lesson in human nature and you don't like it. Being the professional entrepreneur you are, you carry on with your day to day and get on with building your company. You do what you do best and eventually forget about the whole situation.

Then one day, around a year later, you receive an email. The email is from the same chump who sat in your office twelve months ago with the impressive, eager pitch that convinced you to hand over that check. You read on, and the eventual conclusion of the email is that they are asking you for money again. It insinuates that since you gave once, you might want to do it again.

How does this email make you feel?

Are you filled with joy and excitement, or does it bring back all those feelings of resentment you had all those months ago?

Most probably the latter, right?

So what do you do with that email? If you are like most people who have been in this position the email is met with a very swift repositioning into the recycle bin!

You see, if you don't treat the aftermath of the donation as seriously as the initial ask, then you are almost guaranteeing that your donor will be a one timer. Not only that, but the likelihood of them recommending you to anyone else is little to none. Treating the time after the experience for the donor with as much priority, care, and importance as the donation itself is crucial to creating long-standing relationships and expansion of your donor network. The following chapters will show you how to work with your donor in this second and arguably most important stage of fundraising.

GIVEN

CHAPTER TEN

GRATITUDE

How do you show gratitude?

GIVE SOMEONE A GIFT!

What is gratitude?

THE ACT OF BEING GRATEFUL!

Sure, but it is so much more than this. Benedictine Monk David Steindl-Rast suggests that gratitude can be defined by two qualities.

The first of these is **appreciation**, both in terms of appreciating someone and feeling appreciated yourself.

The second is that if it comes **without a price tag**, you do not expect anything in return for your gratitude. Being grateful is the blessing in itself. Gratitude holds no value and is therefore expressed whether the gift received is financial or not.

Many things can be gifted: time, knowledge, energy, networks, and of course, finances. Each one of these is just as valuable as the other, and showing gratitude for those gifts should be done freely.

Gratitude and the act of being grateful are things that are too often overlooked. As humans we have a tendency to see problems or hurdles. If we are successful enough to solve the problem or get over the hurdle, we rarely take time to appreciate that success. We are instead usually looking for the next hurdle to overcome.

The whole *keep rising, keep winning, keep moving forward* attitude is great, but it causes us to miss a fundamental step in our own personal development and the development of relationships with other people. We miss out not only on allowing ourselves to be grateful, but also on learning how to express that gratitude.

Now, as I said previously, gratitude should be given and received freely. When we do allow ourselves to feel grateful, we often reach for our go-to defense mechanisms, especially among successful people. We want to give a gift back. Unfortunately, this act is tainted with ego, and the desired effect can actually backfire.

Imagine spending hours thinking of the perfect gift for your friend. You have been friends for years, and life has taken you down different paths. You have raised a family and lived a relatively simple life, while your friend has gone off to become a high-flying, six-figure executive in New York who parties every night and wears new designer clothes every time you see them. You are still incredibly close friends and arrange to meet up for their birthday, but what do you give to the person who has everything?

You can't afford their fancy luxuries or the material things that they no doubt desire in their life (if they haven't already bought it themselves), so you rack your brain and eventually come up with something amazing, not costly, but creative. You put all the work into making it special. You take them for dinner and surprise them with the amazing gift. They are clearly touched, and you can see how much it means to them. This makes you feel good; you have given them a gift from the heart and taken them for dinner. Perfect. You finish off your crème brûlée, and when your friend heads to the restroom, you ask your waiter for the bill.

"THAT'S OK, MA'AM. YOUR FRIEND ALREADY PAID."

Just then, said friend walks back into the room with a smug smile on their face.

"IT'S THE LEAST I CAN DO FOR THAT AMAZING PRESENT YOU GAVE ME. I KNOW YOU CAN'T REALLY AFFORD THE MEAL, SO THIS ONE'S ON ME!"

While they may think they are doing the right thing here, their right thing has made you feel like crap—if not a bit humiliated to boot. You see, their attempt at gratitude was not done freely and with appreciation. It was a gift with conditions. They felt the need to repay your kind gesture, and in turn it's left you feeling inadequate and worthless.

So how do you express gratitude freely and with appreciation? The first part here is in-credibly underrated—a simple two words: *thank you*. I can imagine everyone reading this right now saying, "Come on! No one takes investments or donations without saying thank you!"

Well, you would be surprised. I once organized a fundraising campaign and gave over $50k each to eleven different charities. Of those eleven, I received a thank-you letter from six, a generic letter sent to all donors with a free pen from two, a handwritten card (this is my personal favorite)from two, and finally one charity who I fundraised and donated $50k to, I never heard a peep—not one single word. I only knew they received it when they cashed the check.

I had a follow-up email from six of the charities, and one of the free pen giver's next contact with me was when they emailed to ask if I would put them in touch with the individuals who donated to my fundraising campaign. Basically, "Can you give me your contact information so we can bypass the middleman [me] and go directly to the source?" This was another addition to the naïveté of this type of fundraiser. They believed that I had simply asked for the donation and they had handed the money over.

Before anyone donates to my causes, I have found out every piece of information available on the person or business. I have followed my MAPS formula and am ready to tackle any questions. Most of the time I have developed long-term relationships with my donors, and I make sure they feel 100 percent special.

So asking me for the contact information of people I have put hours, days, months, and years into building up profiles and relation-ships with is actually a downright insult. It was the very definition of entitlement that I see time and time again in the world of fund-raising (actually in the world in general).

When someone has donated or invested with you and taken that chance, the first thing you do before all else is say *thank you*. Say it, and mean it. Make sure the recipient of your words hears you and that you really look them in the eyes. This stage of gratitude is critical, and you have to use this moment to make them feel like you truly appreciate what they have done. If you take the time to make someone feel special and like they really matter, they will remember that, and they will feel appreciated.

Personally, I find the best form of thank you is straight from the mouth, looking into a person's eyes, and saying it from the heart. A very common way of saying thank you in the charity world, however, is to say it via a letter. This can be effective, but only if done correctly. I have received many forms of thank-you letters, so what is the best kind?

The rule here is simple: the more personalized you can make the letter, the better. At the bottom tier is the generic letter, the one that is received by every donor or supporter. It usually begins with *Dear Supporter of …* or *Dear Sir/Madam …* or, god forbid, *Dear Sir …* This one is highly unappreciated by female executives, by the way.

The next one is the letter in which they've taken time to insert your name and possibly hand sign. This is a great improvement, but for the busy CEO it still stands a risk of ending up in the shredder pile. The better thank-you notes are handwritten cards with personalized thoughts and thank yous. These are the best type to receive and stand less of a chance of hitting the trash.

Now the best of the best thank-you notes are something personalized from the people who have really benefited from the investment or donation. In business, this could be photos of the new premises or the new machine that you have financed. In charity this could be from the kids whose school you have helped build or someone who has received a lifesaving operation. Whatever the cause was, show the donor what their money has truly done and who it has really benefitted. That is the best thank you they can get. I have received posters made by the kids and a montage of letters and videos of children drinking from a well that we funded. All of these examples, even for the hardest of hearts, will be very unlikely to find their way to the trash pile!

Expressing your gratitude publicly is a fantastic way to make your donor feel appreciated. The exception to this lies when the donor or investor has specifically stated they want to remain anonymous. It is incredibly important this request is respected; however, these guys are in the minority, and most people do appreciate the public thanks. This can be done via social media, the press, or even by discussing them at a public event. A donor or investor who has helped make a difference will feel appreciated when you make your gratitude public. A well-constructed social media post or press article can do wonders for your relationship with your donor or investor.

As a point of caution, just be careful depending on what country you are working in. Some countries do not allow certain types of rewards for charity donations. These are usually gray areas, so it's worth taking legal advice on this.

As an example, some countries do not allow gifts in exchange for donations. Gifts *can* be classed as goodwill, which *can* be classed as kudos for the donation. As I say, it can be a gray area and definitely worth investigating and getting a legal sign-off for prior. The very last thing you want is your donor or cause being involved in any type of controversy.

CHAPTER ELEVEN

INFORM

It is human nature to want to avoid uncertainty. We generally like clarity and love to be informed.

Two thousand years ago Marcus Terentius Varro created the nine books of discipline, which is often cited as the template of the encyclopedia. You may be old enough to remember the door-to-door salesmen or the mail order clubs where you could collect encyclopedias and watch your collection grow.

If you were like me (a geek), this excited you!

It was the best way of satisfying my thirst for knowledge. The birth of the internet in the eighties only furthered the testament that humans have a blood-thirsty desire for information. The advent of Google in the nineties helped the internet user shift through a vast array of information to obtain more accurate information. Google quickly became one of the most powerful companies in the world.

It was not long until we were able to discover and share more stories via social media, and the world changed forever. A person's desire for knowledge and to be kept informed is now greater than any time in history, and it is no longer a privilege but a necessity. This desire only increases when the subject matter is close to the person's heart or something they are invested in, and the quickest way for someone to become disheartened is for them to be uninformed.

When people are uninformed, they will generally jump to assumptions and fill in any gaps by themselves. Unfortunately, with very little information, those assumptions can often end as negative ones.

That is not to say you should tell your investor absolutely everything that is going on in your company—the highs, the lows, the good, the bad, and the ugly. No, they don't need all that, but they do need something.

So how do you find the right balance between keeping them informed and oversharing?

Let's answer that with the four Ws:

Where should it be shared?

What should you share with them?

When should you share?

Why are you keeping them informed?

"The **ABSENCE** of **KNOWLEDGE**
evokes the **ABUNDANCE** of **IGNORANCE**,
manifesting in **ASSUMPTIONS**,
carefully disguised as facts of the entitled."

—Alana Stott

WHERE

Let's first look at the where. Most nonprofits, businesses, and influencers operate an emailing system that's designed to keep people up-to-date on the comings and goings of the organization. At one stage this was an incredibly useful tool to share information; however, with more and more organizations doing it, the attention-grabbing strength of the general mailshot is minimal.

In today's world, people are doing all they can to reduce their inboxes. People are waking up to twenty to thirty emails a day, and if you are a CEO or someone heavily involved in multiple fields—or if you are like me—you will easily wake up to two to three *hundred* emails a day. I have systems set up on my accounts that will generally filter out spam and anything that resembles it.

Globally inbox placement rate sits around 80 percent, so one in six end up in the junk box and are never opened. Engagement levels also play a crucial role when companies like Google or Yahoo! are filtering out spam. If previous emails have not been read or were deleted before read, then future emails will most likely be filtered into spam.

If the system doesn't filter it out and you are lucky enough to find your way into the in-box of your donors, then you are faced with manual interaction. If an email in the in-box vaguely resembles junk, then it will be swiftly treated as such. Generic mailing lists usually look like junk mail and will quickly find their way into the trash.

It's our natural instinct to want to filter out anything that looks generic. This is particularly true in the busy world of executives. They often have an assistant whose first job in the morning is to sift through the emails and get rid of any rubbish. If it is not personalized, nothing jumps out, or it looks like junk mail then it will most likely end up in the trash.

Therefore, making your email the least like spam you can is crucial to ensure it is opened and, more importantly, that it is read! This brings us back to personalization. It is very simple to set up personalized emails to each donor. There are many systems now that can do this. Ensuring the email is sent from a specific person, not just the company name, and addressed to a specific person and not just a group.

While email is a great way to reach the masses, many people, believe it or not, do not have access to the internet or just don't care about it. These donors are often of the old-school generation, in which communication was done via letter or a telephone call.

While letters—especially handwritten ones—are a great way to make someone feel appreciated, informed, and individual, another method that is very underused in this day and age is a good old-fashioned phone call. While personal-ized emails are the next best thing to hand-written letters that are slower yet more per-sonal, nothing gives a donor a better feeling than speaking to a real person while being informed.

Remember, the telephone is the tool that once revolutionized the way we communicate. The au-thenticity of this method is only made better by actual human contact. The pandemic of 2020 left many people feeling isolated and lonely. For some the telephone became their only hope of having any contact with the outside world.

For this group of people, feeling appreciated and not forgotten can be the difference between a day of sadness or a day of hope and joy.

Other methods for keeping the donor regularly informed are: informative text messages, press releases, events, and media updates. Whichever method you choose for keeping your donor informed, make sure you do it, and ideally, personalize it!

WHAT

Once you know where and how you are sending your communications, the next important thing to decide is what you should be telling them. It's incredibly important that you don't over-share with potential investors and donors. This is not me saying you should hide important information, or even worse, lie to them, but giving them too much information that is not necessary can complicate the relationship. If what you are sharing is giving you sleepless nights, chances are it will give them sleepless nights too.

Your donor doesn't need a debrief of the entire journey. They just need to know where you are, the destination, and the plan to get there. Fine details and hurdles are not required. It's an incredibly fine line. They need to know you have it under control and that you can be trusted, but they also want to know if you have requirements and if they can help.

There are a number of psychological methods you can use to deliver news and updates, and I'm sure every trainer will swear by a different method. As I am a preacher of positive mindset, I would say this is an important aspect of the delivery. I must stress, however, that positive delivery does not always mean positive news. I hear many leadership gurus and self-help coaches talk about living with a positive mindset, ignoring all the negatives, and all sorts of other cliché hallmark quotes; however, this is not my style.

IN THE WORLD OF MONEY, YOU NEED TO KNOW THE GOOD, THE BAD AND THE UGLY.

You have to deliver to your team and your investors in a way that lets them know all these things too, but in a way that fills them with hope and desire to keep helping and stay vested.

This means you should always start with the good news: the recognition, expressions of gratitude, and what has been achieved. For the "bad" element of the update, maybe a major funding project has been pulled, new legislation has thrown a curve ball, or a fundraiser or investment round wasn't as successful as predicted, how do you address these things?

The main thing is not to bullshit or sugar coat. Address the issue head on, but only if you have a firm solution and lessons learned.

Sharing a problem without the solution is just going to cause concern and nervousness. Tackling the issue head on and having a solution that is following the same methods as the MAPS formula will keep the investor, not only engaged, but increasing in trust because you were willing to share.

Now onto the ugly. These are situations that are out of you or your team's own making, were avoidable, or that could be embarrassing. The same thing follows as it did with the bad—keep it real, but have a solution. The only difference here is, as this was avoidable you need to have an explanation for the instance and a plan to ensure it won't happen again. Once again, the funder will respect the fact that you have been honest. You have identified the issue and have a plan in place to fix it and avoid it happening again.

Finally, always close out with a positive and a call to action. These are the amazing things we are achieving, and this is what we have the potential to do with a bit more help. Remember to finish off with a final expression of gratitude every time.

WHEN

Timing is everything. This is true in business and in donor retention, as it is in life. The timing when it comes to money is very much dependent on the method in which the engagement has been arranged. These methods include:

$ **them coming to you**

$ **invited**

$ **politely invited**

$ **unsolicited**

Social media is a great example of them coming to you. Their visiting you on social media is your chance to really showcase the day-to-day operations of what you do, as well as the highlights of your work. This is your chance to be creative and show your investors why they have chosen to invest in you.

If you have a vested donor, they will want to see something regular on your networks. There are certain times of the day that will capture them more: first thing in the morning, during lunch breaks, and after dinnertime are the usual phone-checking times; however, the dawn of the Covid age paved a way for the constant checkers.

My best advice here is to keep it consistent, keep it entertaining, and if it is possible for you brand or cause, always opt to develop your own brand style, something your supporters can easily identify as *you*. There are several great resources out there on how to get creative and build your brand through social media. Study your options and the reviews before committing to one.

The next group is made up of the ones who have invited you to inform them. I put this into two categories: invited and politely invited. The invited are investors who have specifically requested to be kept informed; they may even stipulate how often, such as a weekly or monthly review. Politely invited are donors who have perhaps joined the mailing list or ticked a box allowing updates.

You must be careful to keep these guys informed but without bombardment. Permission can be removed just as easily as given, and with today's data laws noncompliance with a data removal request can have serious consequences. Most countries have laws on unsolicited mail, especially after a request to stop contact. Therefore, you really want to avoid people unsubscribing by following the content rules in the *what* section.

Equally, if they have asked to be kept informed, ensure you do just that. Every now and then or sporadic messaging will make you seem flaky and erratic. A weekly update with a set day and time will give a sense of consistency, stability, and regularity. If you get the content just right, they will actually look forward to receiving that email.

Finally, and the ones who need handled the most carefully, are the unsolicited or uninvited. These guys should be handled at all times with kid gloves. Uninvited contact is largely taboo, if not forbidden, and if you are asked to stop contacting them you must do so; therefore, when contacting people unsolicited, be careful! You want to make sure they understand who you are, where you're from, and why you are contacting them.

Don't assume they know you just because they have invested. You want to gain their trust and turn them into future invited guests. Once again, this is about making them feel special and as if they are the one and only. You want to be informing them of something new and exciting that will draw their attention. Once you have that attention it will then be your job to keep them.

WHY

This can be broken down into two areas:

1. **Why do the donors want to be kept informed?**
2. **Why are you keeping them informed?**

Your donor wants to be kept informed for a multitude of reasons but mainly because they want to know where their money has gone and what difference it has made.

You want to keep your donor informed as you want to make sure the donor stays invested so that the cycle of giving continues. It really is as simple as that.

It is all about long-term growth. Both in terms of business and relationship, you want both to be ever-evolving and flourishing; therefore, effective communication is key. You should always be learning about your donor, so these communications are a chance to let your donor know that, not only are you thinking of them, but you are staying informed about them too. Simple things like remembering birthdays or key milestones are very useful for building solid relationships. It is always good practice to set google alerts about your major donors.

If the donor, for example, wins an award and you send congratulations before they even have the chance to inform you of this, you will most certainly win brownie points.

Keeping regular communications between you and your donor will also help your team and make their jobs more seamless. Regular updates and data recording will also save time for any future campaigns.

CHAPTER TWELVE

VALUE

Valuing your donor and knowing the value of your donor are two separate things that are equally important. To ensure they feel valued, make sure you invite them to events. Let them be the first to know about things, mention them in posts and websites, send handwritten notes or thank-you cards, and showcase them where you can. Your donor is more valuable to you when they feel valued, so the question of how valuable your donor is to you is answered simply by how valuable you are making them feel.

This goes back to the initial asking for money stage. During the process of trying to obtain the money you made sure to make your donor feel incredible. You worked the MAPS formula to a T, and that is evident by the fact that you have now received the funding.

HOW DID YOU WORK THE MAPS FORMULA?

Was it by endless gifts and over-the-top affirmation about how amazing they were? No. The devil, as they say, was in the details.

I want to give you two examples of people you do business with every day; we all know them.

Let's start with the guy who makes you feel like you are their one-and-only client, who makes you feel like you are Cuba Gooding Junior and he is Tom Cruise in *Jerry Maguire*. He is going to take you as his one-and-only client and you are both going to go all the way!

DO YOU KNOW THAT GUY?

I once had a manager who worked for me for a few years. Over the time we worked together I had come to learn just how important he was and how many high-profile clients he had—names that people would certainly know more than they will mine.

I learned these facts very slowly, as at the time I genuinely would have said that I was his one-and-only client, that he worked only for me, and that it was the two of us against the world. Nothing was ever too much trouble for him. If I called, he answered, and he never had distractions. I now know that all of his many other clients no doubt felt the exact same way as I did.

Then you have the other guy—you know the one. He's always keen to tell you every five minutes just how busy he is and leaves his phone on the table during your catch up (as someone more important than you may be calling at any second). You hear about how he barely has enough hours in the day, how every second is precious—especially these ones he is spending with you, so please hurry up if you can.

Do you have both those guys in your head? Now, when it comes to working with them, to promoting them, and to supporting them in their endeavors, who would you choose?

You are now more than aware they are both busy—though I would guess the first guy has substantially more on his plate but just gets on with it. They are both talented at their job, and are both more than capable of getting the job done. But with the short number of years in business you have, who do you want to work with?

It's a rhetorical question, of course. We all know exactly who people want to work with. This is as true in your business as it is for donors and investors. They don't want to know how many donors you have; they want to know that they are special, they want to feel like the only one, and you need to be ready to treat them as such.

CHAPTER THIRTEEN

ENGAGE

Engaging with your donor and making the conversation a two-way exchange is extremely important when it comes to long-term retention of your donors. Making someone feel part of what the process of what you are doing and making them believe they are an integral part of that process will bring you a long way to a prolonged and sustainable relationship. I always say my goal is to make the donor feel like they are the only donor, they are important, and they are a major part of the team. How to go about this is simple.

SCHEDULE REGULAR CHECK-INS, AND KNOW YOUR DONOR.

Track the data, and make sure you and your team are kept informed about your donor. Knowing little things like their birthday or their kids' names can be a game changer. Engaging with your investor will keep them engaged with you. It is no different to any other relationship. It takes work, effort, and the occasional bunch of flowers!

Events are a fantastic tool to keep them engaged. This doesn't have to be an all-singing, all-dancing, red carpet, celebrity-filled ceremony. They can be simple on-site events where you show them around and let them immerse themselves in their investment. As said previously, everyone wants to know where their money has gone, and the more positive the vibe they are feeling during this, the better for them and for you. Be sure to personalize their invites and customize the invites to the occasions. Have fun with it, and make being involved with you an enjoyable process.

If you are active on social media, be sure to include your donors. Tag them in anything new and exciting. Don't just stick to things about you, your business, or your cause. If your donor has shared something exciting, be sure to build them up. Share their stories and updates, and make them feel you care about them just as much as you want them to care about you. Mutual praise and encouragement will not only make everyone feel good, but it will also increase your own visibility and encourage other people to join in what you are doing.

Being kind and supportive really is always a win-win situation.

Encourage your investors to take part in what you are doing. I once had a sponsor join me on an emergency trip where I had to move two vehicles from Florida, USA, to Panama City, Panama—eight countries in seven days—in order to keep a fundraising challenge moving. The investor flew to Florida with me where we met with the team and collected the two vehicles. We drove through Mexico, Guatemala, Honduras, Nicaragua, and Costa Rica before arriving in Panama. We were faced with everything from being held at gunpoint in Honduras to corrupt bribery from border agent police in Costa Rica.

It was a dangerous and worrying trip; however, once it was complete and everyone was home safe, it was a bond that's hard to break.

THEY WERE SERIOUSLY INVESTED IN MAKING THE FUNDRAISING CHALLENGE A SUCCESS AS THEY HAD NOW WITNESSED IT FIRSTHAND.

They truly were engaged and remained that way throughout the campaign and beyond.

CHAPTER FOURTEEN

NETWORK

Now you have your donor. You have gained their trust, their affection, and their buy-in. But there is one thing they have left that you want—no actually—that you need—

THEIR NETWORK!

When building a business, fundraising, or seeking investment, a strong network and pool of connections is crucial. Your network should be an ever-evolving and expanding part of your business and prioritized at all times. You need to be engaging with all your donors to get them to open up their little black book to you. If you have put into practice all the other tools in this book, then this part should be very easy for you.

Your donors should be your biggest supporters and want to talk about you. They want to shout about you, and they won't stop at that. They should be so impressed they want to encourage others to join you too. If they haven't done it already, then do not be afraid to ask.

A well-respected and well-engaged donor should have no issues at all with opening up their network to you, and if they don't, then this is a problem you need to resolve as a matter of priority. If they do agree, then give them that nudge to do so. Offer to speak at their events or host parties for them. If they have donated, it's likely their circle will too.

A good network is not only vital to the success of your campaign, but it will also help you to grow. It will allow you to see future trends such as company CSRs (corporate social responsibilities) and where investors are placing their funding. It will strengthen your business and fundraising connections in the community and wider reach.

HAVE YOU EVER HEARD THE SAYING YOU LEARN NOTHING BY TALKING?

Networking is all about listening to other people and soaking up as much information from them as possible. The more people in your network, the greater the chance of diversity and wider-reaching ideas.

As your network grows, you have more opportunities to branch out your divisions. You will be able to identify the qualities of your network and how each person can benefit the various stages of your fundraising journey.

If, for example you have a particularly large pool of high-profile, celebrity, or large-following influencers on your list, then these are the perfect people for promotions or events. Encouraging them to share what you have going on with their followers will give you a huge increase in visibility, and if you are looking to increase the followers of your cause, there is no better way than utilizing influencers' existing lists.

The golden rule here is: *Keep your ink dry.* If you over-ask people to make introductions, to share posts, or to promote your brand, then you will stand the risk of generosity burn out. People do not like to feel used. You have to follow the **how to ask for money rules,** even with your promotional asks.

SUMMARY

$ Always show gratitude.

$ Say thank you.

$ Personalize your response—the more personalized the better.

$ Keep your donors informed and up to date at all times.

$ Go out of your way to make investors feel valued.

$ Stay engaged and engage your donors to make them feel special.

$ Evolve and expand your network at every opportunity.

PART FOUR
EXTRAS

CHAPTER FIFTEEN

PLANNING A GALA FUNDRAISER

"THIS IS THE PART EVERYONE LOVES!

It has to be the most exciting part of fund-raising, the fun part—the time to drink, party, and feel good!"

SAID NO EVENT PLANNER EVER!

Planning a fundraising event is quite simply hard work! There are no airs and graces when it comes to this statement. It's long hours, stressful calls, heads banging against walls, and general breakdown-style exhaustion.

I BASICALLY LIKEN IT TO GOING THROUGH LABOR.

It's painful and exhausting for you, while everyone else around you enjoys the magical miracle that is unfolding before their eyes—the birth of your baby. But once it's complete and you're holding that baby in your arms, looking at what you have created, well it's a pretty amazing feeling, and all the pain slowly disappears.

Event planning, much like growing a baby, is a long process that cannot and should not be rushed. Creating a life takes nine months from concept to development, and I would use that as a good minimum benchmark for planning an event.

I have had people tell me they can pull off the fundraiser of the century within a matter of a couple of months, or even worse, a few weeks. Well, much like everything else I have discussed in the book, event planning cannot be rushed. It takes management, accountability, planning, and strategy.

IT TAKES MAPS!

The MAPS formula can be adapted to most financial asks, including event planning.

LET ME SHOW YOU HOW!

Using MAPS will ensure you have a successful event, no matter what you are doing, but there are a few extra specifics we can apply to running a one-off fundraising gala event as opposed to a longer-running campaign. For a number of organizations, the annual fundraiser is their one and only time of the year to bring money into their organization[*], so the gala event really is make or break for them. Therefore, getting it right and bringing in as much money as possible is everything.

But back to the event. Let's look at how we can adapt and add to the MAPS formula to make it more specific to your event. When looking specifically at event planning, I change the M from mindset, to management. While mindset is still a big factor in planning a gala, I feel adapting the M to management is required for this type of event planning. I would advise you to still review the mindset aspect of the formula too but for now lets look at management.

---

[*] *I will also note that this is not the ideal financial plan for a nonprofit, and if this is your set-up then you need get in touch with me to fix this ASAP!*

MANAGEMENT

Whether you decide to plan the event your-self or bring in a seasoned event planner, I strongly advise you to never relinquish con-trol of the event or anything that is involved in the lead-up to the event.

Taking control of the management of an event involves:

$ developing the budget

$ managing location and venue selection requisites

$ managing the logistics

$ creating the theme and ensuring its achievable for all

$ staff management

$ vendor management

$ contract negotiations

$ conflict management

$ fundraising management

$ table management

$ donor management

$ catering management

$ talent management

$ managing the to-do list

$ managing invitations and guest list

$ entertainment management

$ auction management

$ post-event management

As you can see, a huge amount of event management is during the actual event itself. Most of the prework falls more into the planning section.

Managing an event from start to finish is a process that can take over a year. If you are in charge of the management, be sure to know what is happening in every aspect of your event plan, and don't be afraid to ask for help!

ACCOUNTABILITY

Planning a gala fundraiser is all about knowing exactly how to ask for money; therefore, accountability is more important than ever. The result of every single one of your actions will be seen immediately, and if you get any step of it wrong, you cannot change the outcome.

THE BUCK TRULY AND FULLY STOPS WITH YOU.

You must be accountable for every stage of the management, planning, and strategy, including any delegation of responsibilities. Some of the important questions you should know the answers to are:

WHAT IS THE EVENT FOR?

Know exactly what the cause is, and if you are raising for more than one cause, make sure you fully understand all the causes and how they complement or conflict each other. Be sure to be able to communicate this with your guests and donors.

WHO ARE THE BENEFICIARIES?

Who will actually benefit from what happens during the evening? Don't just know the charity names, but know exactly who the funds are going to, as you most definitely *will* be asked!

HOW WILL THEY BENEFIT SPECIFICALLY?

How will they benefit? Is there something specific the funds are helping with, such as funding the opening of a new wing of a hospital or building a school?

WHAT ARE THE EXPECTED FINANCIAL OUTCOMES?

How much is needed in order for the benefit to happen, and if the amount is not hit, what happens? People want to know what the expectations are, and it will also encourage them to be a part of reaching that goal. A donor loves to be the one who makes you reach your goal!

Make sure you know the full amount, including cost of benefit and all the overheads involved in the event and planning.

WHO ARE THE KEY MEMBERS OF YOUR TEAM?

When it comes to selecting the team, the staff, the committee, and so forth, be sure to know what skills are required and what skills each person has at hand. Be sure that you are transparent about it. If you are bringing someone onto your committee due to your knowledge of their little black book, be sure to tell them that is why. There is no point bringing them on if they have no intention of ever opening their book to you. Being honest and upfront is key.

WHO ARE YOUR ATTENDEES?

Why do you need to know who is on your guest list? I have organized events at the Gleneagles Hotel in Scotland, the Grosvenor Hotel in London, and the local pub in Ireland, and one thing they all have in common? The guest list was key.

Where you have the event is all a matter of geography and aesthetics; however, if you don't have the right people in the room, you will not hit your target. Don't assume the right people means the rich people. I have seen the local hairdresser become the biggest bidder for the night and the Russian billionaire walk out, leaving someone else to settle the bill.

Knowing your guest list is also very useful for planning your auction. Putting two opposing companies on the tables next to each other is always a good plan for encouraging competitive bidding!

PLANNING

The to-do list for planning an event is very similar to the list involved in management, with the very subtle differences between the words *management* and *planning*. They may seem the same, but they are very different, with the clue in the words!

THE SECRET TO SMOOTH MANAGEMENT IS EFFECTIVE PLANNING.

If you can perfect the planning stage, it will make the management of an event seamless and even enjoyable.

"**BEFORE** anything else, **PREPARATION** is *the key* to **SUCCESS**."

—Alexander Graham Bell

The time you spend during the planning phase is rarely wasted. My first advice when it comes to planning an event is to form a committee. These people should become your event-planning dream team. Don't try and do it all on your own. Yes, the buck stops with you, but that doesn't mean you should do it all on your own.

The most important thing when forming a committee is to be varied, diverse, and have members with a wide range of skills, backgrounds, and abilities. This should not be a box-ticking exercise. This should be about selecting the right people who will enhance the team and make it multi-faceted. People to consider bringing on board are:

- people with a wide network of friends and business contacts
- influencers with high follower counts
- people with financial backgrounds
- creative individuals
- administrators
- skilled sales negotiators
- skilled arts professions such as videographers and tech

Once the committee is formed and in place, be sure to meet on a regular basis and treat each meeting like a business board meeting. Have someone take the minutes for every meeting, and set out clear instructions and tasks for each person. Make sure you lay out your key objectives for the event, and lay out how you plan to achieve them.

If you are planning to raise one million dollars, set out how you plan to do this. And be specific.

Examples would be:

$ Target $1,000,000.

$ Raised through auction $500,000. Ten auction items minimum $50k per item.

$ Tables available 50, sell at $10k per table, total income $500,000.

This list can be endless, but be sure to capture it all. Once you know your objectives, then you have to delegate to the right people. Ensure you make this stage interactive. You don't want people agreeing to tasks that they are unsure if they can achieve.

My other piece of advice when it comes to event planning is:

EFFECTIVE TIME MANAGEMENT IS YOUR BEST FRIEND!

I have rarely attended an event (except my own) that starts on time, doesn't run over on speech times, doesn't go on too late, or that runs according to schedule!

The time planning of an event is often overlooked, but that is the biggest turn-off for your attendees. I promise you the last thing you want come auction time is a whole load of bored attendees.

STRATEGY

As discussed earlier, it is incredibly diffi-cult to manage a full event by yourself. Your committee should now be helping you form the strategy as to how you will implement all the steps.

Developing your strategy around event planning is done in the exact same way as you would when you are developing a strategy on asking for money, with one key addition.

PREPARING FOR IMPULSE BUYING

Adapting an impulse buying plan into your strategy is extremely important for a gala event. You will be relying on pulling at heart-strings and getting immediate buy-in when it comes to auctions, bidding, and getting your audience to instantly part with their cash!

Impulse buying planning is different to the sales planning I previously discussed. In these circumstance, such as auctions, you are re-lying on the sell-me-the-pen method; however, that is not to say it should all be impro-vised. You can still strategize and plan how to optimize your chances of maximum success. This is all about forming an **auction-specific strategy plan** (ASSP).

It is not only recommended to form an ASSP, it is, in my opinion, a **MUST**!

MINIMAL

UNOBTAINABLE

SIMPLE

TIMING

Keeping the auction *minimal* will attract and keep your audience's attentions. I would rarely advise over ten auction items, and even that might be too much. I prefer to keep the auction items for the main auction to around five to seven lots.

Make your items *unobtainable*. They should be money-can't-buy tickets. If a person is able to buy it, they are rarely likely to pay over the value for it. People want something they would otherwise never be able to obtain, such as dinner with a celebrity or staying at a venue that normal Joe is not permitted to, like the White House!

Keep the items sharp and *simple*. When they are overcomplicated or difficult to understand, you will lose your audience's attention. Keep the items simple, understandable, and easy.

Timing is everything when kicking off an auction. At the very beginning of the evening, your guests will be too rigid and somewhat shy. By the end of the evening, the wine has not only taken effect, but has sent many over the edge. A lot may have left, but most want to dance, and attention spans are gone.

Halfway through the evening is ideal, when everyone has loosened up. Your host should prepare the room for the auction and immediately before the auction is when you want to be showing any heartstring-pulling videos. You really want to be getting them ready to open their wallets either by tearjerkers or guilt complexes.

To conclude, a fundraising event is very similar to asking for money in general, following the same rules, and applying the MAPS formula with a few adjusts will give you the best chance a successful event that can hopefully have you forming a waitlist for your next event!

"Give me **SIX HOURS** to **CHOP** down a tree and I will spend the **FIRST FOUR** *sharpening the* **AXE**."

—Abraham Lincoln

CHAPTER SIXTEEN

HOW TO ASK FOR FREE STUFF

There are times when what you need is not cold hard cash. Sometimes you need things or supplies; you need stuff!

Think of the red-carpet gala event, and think of your budget. A lot of the costs involved in running a gala are the supplies. Of course you can try to find sponsors to cover the costs of your supplies, but what if you could get them for free?

WHAT WOULD FREE SUPPLIES MEAN FOR YOUR CAUSE?

Well, it would likely mean that all the funds you are raising will go directly to the cause and not to overheads. Just like it is in business, the fewer expenses you have, the more money goes to profit.

So how do you ask suppliers to provide you products for free, or even better,

GET THEM TO PAY YOU TO ALLOW THEM TO GIVE YOU THE PRODUCTS FOR FREE?

What? Did I write that wrong? Do I really think people will give you their products, not only for free, but they will also pay you to allow them to give you their products?

YES, I DID SAY THAT, AND I DON'T JUST THINK THIS TO BE TRUE—I KNOW IT!

Everyday, celebrities are paid by brands to simply accept their gifts. They don't have to do an advertising campaign or actively go out and promote the brand. All they have to do is casually be seen wearing the clothes or holding the bag, and that is enough for them to be paid for receiving the free gift. This may sound crazy, but it is incredibly smart marketing. It isn't an ad or an obvious paid promotion. It is casual, it is everyday, and it seems so much more authentic than the commercials.

OK, so I know your fundraising idea or investment pitch is no Kim Kardashian, but it is a commodity to people and can be equally exploited in order to bring in more funds.

Let me explain in more detail. If you are hosting a black-tie event benefitting juvenile diabetes, the event itself will most likely be attended by people who have purchased the ticket because this is a cause they want to support. Perhaps they want to support it for personal reasons, or it could be this is a business decision, or it may just be they very much enjoy supporting charities.

Whatever the reason, they are there because they trust your cause's brand and want to help and support it. Therefore, the product placement around the room will be noticed by them.

If I say a champagne company donated twenty-five cases of bubbles and each person in the room enjoys a glass knowing it was kindly donated, then that company will become appealing to these guests. They have a connection immediately, as they are both there supporting the same cause. It is likely, therefore, that they will notice the brand name, and after the event, they may wish to go buy a few bottles for home.

BUBBLY THAT SUPPORTS A CAUSE—WHAT'S NOT TO LOVE?

If every person in the room feels the same and they tell their friends about it, then the champagne company is in for some really big and frequent sales from their new fan club. Now, to some, that is worth giving away free stuff, but to others it is also worth that extra investment in paying for the opportunity to be involved, give away their products, and attract new clients.

In general, you are applying the same principals as you would in all financial asks. You need to put in the research for the most part, but when it comes to asking for stuff, there is no shame in a blanket approach. You can be a bit bolder here and spread the net wide. I have been gifted everything from free manicures to five-star world cruises.

All I had to do was ask!

If you are asking for someone to provide you with their services for free, be sure to once again apply the MAPS formula, specifically the **what's in it for them section**. Small businesses in particular will want to help, but they will need to know it makes commercial sense for them, and you should always be able to answer the *how* for them.

When asking for money or asking for free stuff the secret is to be prepared. Be ready to answer anything, and be confident in your ask. And finally, make room! Correctly applied, you will soon be receiving as much free stuff as you ask for, and you will need to make some room in your garage for storage!

CHAPTER SEVENTEEN

HOW TO DRESS

As we discussed earlier in your introduction to MAPS, the approach is the key element of success. The first element of relationship building, and the introduction can make, break, enhance or hinder a deal.

FIRST IMPRESSIONS REALLY ARE EVERYTHING.

If you are reading this book, you are probably in the sales, investing or fundraising business, and you will be well-versed in the **first-impression rules**.

THE RULE OF TWELVE

The first twelve seconds, the first twelve words, the first twelve inches from the shoulders up, the first twelve steps taken as a person approaches, these are all classed as deal makers or breakers.

So where better to open discussions about first impressions than with what you should wear? There have been many books written about the importance of what you wear to create the best first impressions.

WHAT YOU WEAR IS OF CRITICAL IMPORTANCE, RIGHT?

I would argue that, really, the truth is, it's all about **you**, your personality, how well you pitch, and how deeply invested you are in your product.

Let's take the last few years as an example—the Covid years. The majority of people in 2020 and 2021 conducted most of their business in their pajama bottoms. While we generally never saw this, it was widely accepted that this was standard practice. We looked good from the waist up and had on soft socks and pants from the waist down.

Did this stop business deals going through? I don't believe I have heard of an example where someone didn't go ahead with a business deal because the associate was wearing fluffy slippers.

My intelligence and investigations business saw an increase in inquiries at an unprecedented rate, especially in regard to the background check and knowing your customer information. When I asked one of my clients, an investor, why he was using these services more he told me that, prior to Covid he would never have made an investment or accepted an investment without first having met the person. He said he needed to feel their energy, gain that first impression, and rely on his primitive gut instincts. Online video calling has taken away that human connection and close energy fields, so we are now finding other ways to get to know a person. We have realized that what a person is wearing is not an indication of if they are a trusted person or someone we would wish to do business with.

It is about respecting the situation, ensuring the first impression is the best it can possibly be, and allowing your positive energy to flow. If you are able to be there in person, concentrate on how you enter the room, your stance, your smile, your hand position, and how you make them feel in those first few minutes. For all this to be optimized you must first feel confident. If a dark-gray business suit is not your thing and will make you feel uncomfortable then don't wear it.

IF YOU FEEL UNCOMFORTABLE, IT WILL SHOW.

Be aware of the environment, but be comfortable, be relaxed, and be ready to ask for what you want, dressed however you feel your most confident.

CHAPTER EIGHTEEN

KNOW YOUR VALUE, KNOW YOUR WORTH

What are you worth?

What is your value?

Is your time an asset?

Are you an asset?

Throughout this book I have done my best to share with you as much of the knowledge I have gained over my years of asking for money as possible, but there is one thing we haven't delved into yet:

YOU.

You can take every piece of information in this book and put it into practice, and yes, it will most definitely improve your chances

of success. However, three of the most fundamental principles of success are

BELIEVING IN YOURSELF, KNOWING YOUR VALUE, AND KNOWING YOUR WORTH.

If you are lacking in these principals, then it will be very hard for your achieve your full potential.

I have worked with people from all walks of life including, Special Forces operators, top TV executives, CEOs of Fortune 500 companies, charity founders, celebrities, and royalty. When working on improving their skills, especially when their struggles were asking for money, there is one thing they all have in common: They all lacked the confidence to express their own value.

I have worked with tier-one Special Forces soldiers who save lives on a daily basis, who would literally take a bullet for people and place a blanket of freedom over us every day; however, when I asked them to put a price tag on what they do they could not give me an answer.

THEY HATED THE IDEA OF CHARGING A HIGH PRICE FOR SOMETHING THEY WOULD SEE AS AN EVERYDAY THING.

What they do as a way of life, most people have only seen in Ridley Scott movies, but to them it is what they call normal life. To them helping people, saving people, and taking a bullet for someone if needed is what they are here for. It comes easily to them. The thought of a mundane nine to five life is what's terrifying to them.

They often go from protecting our country to working in the world of protecting high net worth individuals and celebrities. It's a natural progression. However, they rarely understand the business or celebrity world that their clients are immersed in. In a former Special Forces operator's past career, the daily tasks in the job description involved them literally putting their lives in the hands of their colleagues. There is no room for doubt, reminders, or questioning. Trust between these guys is just a given. The price tag of doing their job is valued at someone's life.

However, there comes a time they have to leave the service and all the millions of dollars that their respective governments have spent training them to become the most highly skilled operators in the world is now for the benefit of the civilian world. But how do you quantify your worth when your previous value was human life? Add to the mix that you are now dealing with people more used to fighting in the boardroom than the battlefield, most of whom would never lose a night's sleep for their colleagues let alone lose their lives.

It is very difficult to navigate this new world, and a particular operator I was working with found it very difficult to place value on himself. He was now in private security and helping some of the most wealthy but vulnerable people in the world. When I reviewed his last few jobs, he had not sent an invoice to at least half of his completed contracts. I asked him what had happened, showing him one example of the missed invoices. He explained that the task was time critical. He had to achieve something in a very short timescale in order to keep the client safe, and he had not had time to discuss fees and rates. The mission was to keep the client safe, so he set his plan into action immediately, putting money to the end of his priorities.

It goes without saying that he achieved his objectives and ensured the clients immediate and ongoing safety, and his mission was complete. But then there came a time that he had to charge for his services. He had been so concerned with the first objective, which to him was the number one priority, preservation of life, that the second objection, payment of services, took a back seat.

THE MAJORITY OF THE BUSINESS WORLD WOULD NOT EVEN BEGIN THIS MISSION WITHOUT FIRST SECURING THE RATES, SCOPE OF WORKS, AND CONTRACT.

Many would take advantage of the critical situation and ask for even more money than they normally would knowing the client is desperate. But for someone like my client, someone who had taken oaths, who had integrity running through his veins and valued life and keeping people safe above all else, valuing himself in monetary terms was next to impossible for him. To him the mission was complete and invoicing the customer just didn't feel right.

Other clients who he did attempt to invoice after the fact would tell him his price was steep and that they pay less than that for their professional and executive team. The respect level was high enough to put their life in this guy's hands, but not enough to pay the operator what he was really worth.

Breaking this all down to enable him to understand his own value and his worth was not an easy task. My own morals and ethics completely understood where his head was, and I fully respected that, but he had to understand that he was no longer on the battlefield. He was in the business world now, and the client in point would have absolutely no hesitation in invoicing anyone for any work he does. He never got to this stage in his career—the stage he needs to hire this operator as a bodyguard—by not understanding his own value and worth.

I BEGAN TO BREAK IT DOWN WITH HIM.

What would have happened if he had not completed his mission?

What would the consequences have been?

Loss of life?

What are the consequences of that?

Children without a father?

Wife without a husband?

Business without a leader?

I continued.

What would the value of this be to that client?

What price tag would this billionaire client place on the value of his life?

The task was not easy, but eventually we broke it all down until he understood just how much he was undervaluing himself.

Now, don't get me wrong, he still struggles with placing monetary value on his services, but he now has an assistant who does all his bidding for him. To this day he has not had a client who has rejected his fee.

His assistant ensures that once the task is agreed, she issues the contract and invoice. The client, who is desperate for this guy's help, always pays. **The respect is up front.** He has something they need, and they value it. Trying to ask for it at the back end when the client no longer needs that service, they no longer value this service, and they have forgotten the threat is much harder. They are safe and the threat has gone, but the respect level has also dropped. When they needed his help, he was god to them, but now they are safe, **they see them as the chump they can get freebies from** because they can see that the operator has not valued himself upfront.

KNOWING YOUR VALUE, KNOWING YOUR WORTH DOES NOT MAKE YOU GREEDY, MONEY HUNGRY, OR COLD-HEARTED. IT MAKES YOU EVEN BETTER AT WHAT YOU DO.

When you know exactly what you are capable of, stand in front of the client eye-to-eye, and say, "You need this service. I am the best person at doing it, and this is what you will need to pay for it."

You may not be guaranteed the contract or job, but you will be guaranteed respect. If they turn you down or frown upon the price, this is not because you are not worth it. It's because they cannot afford you, and that is perfectly OK.

You may now be asking, *If they cannot afford me, should I reduce my price to accommodation them?*

This is an interesting question.

The answer is completely up to you. Now that you know and understand your value, are you willing to compromise and undervalue yourself just to secure a job? Will that help you in the long run? Is it worth it? Only you can really answer that, but if you want my two cents, when you discover your value and your worth, don't compromise. If they want you and need you, it is up to them to find a way to make it happen.

CONCLUSION

HOW TO ASK FOR MONEY— ARE YOU NOW A PRO?

Are you now a master of fundraising?

Are you now an expert in everything there is to know about how to ask for money?

How do you know when you've become a pro at fundraising?

For all the questions and answers we have looked at in this book, this is one of the easiest to address.

THERE IS NO SUCH THING AS 100 PERCENT COMPLETE KNOWLEDGE ON ANY SUBJECT!

Always be smart enough to know what you don't know, and never stop learning. There's great power in accepting that you don't know everything and knowing what you don't know. The smartest people in the world know there is no such thing as knowing everything, no such thing as perfection, and every day they continue to surround themselves with people with more knowledge than them.

An expert is someone who has a vast amount of knowledge on a particular subject, but what separates the professionals and the leaders is consistency—continuously striving to be better than your expert peers. This is how you produce results.

WHAT DO I MEAN BY THIS?

I mean don't make this the last book you read. If something in this book was of particular interest to you, then go out and learn more about that subject. Never stop learning. There isn't a day that goes by when I don't learn something new about the art of fundraising, and in ten years' time, I am sure I could write an entirely new or updated and adapted version of this book.

The knowledge that I have built over the years is what I wanted to pass on in this book. But I would argue that the vast amount of experience I have in asking for money may have been outweighed by everything I learned during the process of researching and writing this book.

THE NEVER-ENDING JOURNEY OF KNOWLEDGE BUILDING

If I had to condense this conclusion based on the original statement in the book title into a few short sentences, they would be:

Embrace your fears.

Preparation is key.

Know your ask.

Respect your donors.

Follow the steps, never stop building your knowledge, and do everything with purpose.

Finally, I want to thank you for coming on this journey with me. This truly has been my labor of love, and I sincerely hope this book has helped you in your fundraising journey.

WHAT YOU DO FOR YOURSELF DIES WITH YOU. WHAT YOU DO FOR OTHERS IS IMMORTAL.

BE INSPIRED

I want to leave you with some of the most inspirational quotes that have inspired me along the way.

"WHEN WE HELP OURSELVES, WE FIND MOMENTS OF HAPPINESS. WHEN WE HELP OTHERS, WE FIND LASTING FULFILLMENT."

—Simon Sinek, best-selling author, TED talker, and eternal optimist

"THE MOST EFFECTIVE WAY TO DO IT, IS TO DO IT."

—Amelia Earhart, pioneer, author, and first female aviator to fly solo across the Atlantic

"I WOULD ASK YOU TO QUESTION WHO'S AT THE TABLE AND WHO'S NOT AT THE TABLE AND TO THINK ABOUT THOSE VOICES THAT AREN'T REPRESENTED WHEN YOU'RE MAKING DECISIONS."

—James Halliday, board chair at Emerging Practitioners in Philanthropy

"SOME PEOPLE WANT IT TO HAPPEN, SOME WISH IT WOULD HAPPEN, OTHERS MAKE IT HAPPEN."

—Michael Jordan, American former pro basketball player and businessman

"DON'T TELL US ALL THE REASONS THIS MIGHT NOT WORK. TELL US ALL THE WAYS IT COULD WORK."

—John Wood, founder of Room to Read

"THE CHALLENGE OF LEADERSHIP IS TO BE STRONG, BUT NOT RUDE; BE KIND, BUT NOT WEAK; BE BOLD, BUT NOT BULLY; BE THOUGHTFUL, BUT NOT LAZY; BE HUMBLE, BUT NOT TIMID; BE PROUD, BUT NOT ARROGANT; HAVE HUMOR, BUT WITHOUT FOLLY."

—Jim Rohn, American entrepreneur, author, and motivational speaker

"LET US REMEMBER: ONE BOOK, ONE PEN, ONE CHILD, AND ONE TEACHER CAN CHANGE THE WORLD."

—Malala Yousafzai, youngest recipient of the Nobel peace prize, activist, and cofounder of Malala Fund

"AN INVESTMENT IN KNOWLEDGE PAYS THE BEST INTEREST."

—Benjamin Franklin, a polymath, writer, philosopher, and founding father of America

"THE ONLY THING STANDING BETWEEN YOU AND YOUR GOAL IS THE BULLSHIT STORY YOU KEEP TELLING YOURSELF AS TO WHY YOU CAN'T ACHIEVE IT."

—Jordan Belfort, entrepreneur, speaker, author and the wolf of Wall Street

"THE BEST WAY TO FIND YOURSELF IS TO LOSE YOURSELF IN THE SERVICE OF OTHERS."

—Mahatma Gandhi, leader of India's independence movement, famous for his philosophy of nonviolence

"WE CANNOT THINK OF BEING ACCEPTABLE TO OTHERS UNTIL WE HAVE FIRST PROVEN ACCEPTABLE TO OURSELVES."

—Malcolm X, human rights activist and prominent figure in the civil rights movement

"I WILL TELL YOU HOW TO BECOME RICH. CLOSE THE DOORS. BE FEARFUL WHEN OTHERS ARE GREEDY. BE GREEDY WHEN OTHERS ARE FEARFUL."

—Warren Buffett, American business magnate, investor, and philanthropist

"EVERYTHING IN LIFE IS A SALE AND EVERYTHING YOU WANT IS A COMMISSION."

—Grant Cardone, best-selling author, trainer, and entrepreneur

"I'VE LEARNED THAT YOU SHOULDN'T GO THROUGH LIFE WITH A CATCHER'S MITT ON BOTH HANDS. YOU NEED TO BE ABLE TO THROW SOMETHING BACK."

—Maya Angelou, poet, memoirist, and civil rights activist

"SO PLEASE ASK YOURSELF: WHAT WOULD I DO IF I WEREN'T AFRAID? AND THEN GO DO IT!"

—Sheryl Sandberg, COO Meta, philanthropist, and best-selling author

"I AM NOT A PROFESSIONAL COACH, BUT I BELIEVE BEING HEALTHY INSIDE AND OUT AND CLEANSING YOUR DEMONS. IT HELPS YOU PERFORM BETTER IN BUSINESS AND BECOME A MORE POSITIVE PERSON."

—Baroness Michelle Mone, entrepreneur, inventor, and founder of MJM International Ltd.

"ALWAYS PLAN AHEAD, IT WASN'T RAINING WHEN NOAH BUILT THE ARK."

—Richard Cushing

"WHEN YOU HAVE GREATER THINGS TO CONCERN YOURSELF WITH, THE OPINION OF IGNORANCE CAN'T PHASE YOU."

"WORK WHILE THEY SLEEP AND ACHIEVE THINGS THAT THEY WILL ONLY DREAM OF."

"IF YOU WANT IT WORK FOR IT, THE TIME YOU PUT IN AT THE BEGINNING WILL DELIVER THREEFOLD IN THE END."

—Alana Stott

ACKNOWLEDGMENTS

One sunny afternoon I was chatting with a business colleague who was a very well-respected, successful, and sought-after business advisor. As we spoke, he mentioned a proposal he was preparing for another client and the prospect that he may have to ask for an increase in fees.

"I HATE THIS PART," HE TOLD ME.

I looked at him, astonished. How could someone so distinguished in their role fear asking for money? When I questioned him about this, he told me, "Alana, it's not just me, asking for money is one of the number one things that cause my clients anxiety. Are you telling me you don't get nervous asking for money?"

"No," I said.

We looked at each other for a while, and it was in that moment I decided to write this book.

Following that moment and to this day I speak to people regularly who tell me about that same fear and anxiousness, and every time I spoke with them, I wanted to get this book out there and help them.

From that initial conversation it has taken over a year to complete this book. There have been ups, downs, and even my own doubts and fears crept in. Luckily, I had this book to refer to in times of turmoil.

Completing the book was a surreal feeling for me, due to both the labor of love and the knowledge that it would soon be out there helping all those people I had spoken to: the charities desperate for funding, the young start-up with no idea how to start the ask, and the ones with genuine crippling fears of going in the room and asking for money. What an amazing feeling to know I could help.

These are the kinds of incredible reactions I've received when I tell people about this book.

"YOU'RE WRITING A BOOK, WHAT'S IT CALLED?"

"HOW TO ASK FOR MONEY."

"OH MY GOD, I NEED THAT BOOK IN MY LIFE!"

Believe me when I say I have spoken to people from every walk of life—from CEOs to students, teachers to entrepreneurs, celebrities to even children—and they all want to know the secret. I am more than happy to share it. If more people with big dreams, hopes, and ideas could take that next step to realizing their ambitions and stop letting the little things like asking for money hold them back, imagine how many new initiatives, innovations, and world changers could be out there. It felt like my duty to share the knowledge far and wide, and this book will hopefully do that—or at the very least provide an informative read!

I cannot end without saying a special thank you to every person along my journey who taught me valuable lessons—the good the bad and the ugly. Not every lesson is easy or understandable at first, but every experience is a chance to grow, to develop, and to learn. I made the choice early on to never stop learning, even when I have had the worst of teachers, even when you think the education in that moment is pointless, there is always something to take from it, even if it's just the what not to dos.

This book really is truly for all those who have helped and inspired me along the way. To everyone who has shared their stories, to my home team, to my work team, to my fabulous friends, and most of all, to my amazing family.

To my husband, Dean, thank you for your support, understanding, and patience during this journey. To my wonderful daughter, Mollie, never let the fear win. To my legendary son, Tommy, keep being your funny fearless self, and to baby Harley, you were growing in my tummy as I was creating this book, and I love that you will always be part of this journey.

You guys all inspire me every day.

Never stop being who you all are, and always know that I do what I do every day for each and every one of you.

All my love, Alana xx